What Other
about t

MW00831406

Grace's moving memoir uses the apt analogy of a seed saver to describe how the experiences of her early years as a missionary and mother of four in Guatemala prepared her for subsequent challenges. When Witness for Peace launched its multi-faith nonviolent movement to stand with the Central Americans, Grace drew upon her stores of courage, faith, and a sense of justice to play a critical leadership role. Those saved seeds brought forth wise guidance for our work with delegations and communities. Now, all of her readers can benefit from this warm narrative of her amazing life of service to her faith, family, and community.

> — Betsy Crites,
> former Executive Director of Witness for Peace

What constitutes a faithful life? There are many answers to that question. But few people exemplify the faithful life like Grace Gyori. As a member of Lake View Presbyterian Church for more than three decades, her role as elder, mentor, teacher and friend to many was that of bellwether for justice. When it felt like there wasn't possibly one more ounce of energy for another issue or problem to solve in the city or the world, Grace had a gentle, yet firm way of reminding us who we were as God's beloved, and that the calling out of injustice always had first claim on any pool of resources. Read this memoir and feel the commitment of a servant, honest and vulnerable, authentic and real. A remarkable telling of a remarkable life.

> With many thanks for her role in making me a better pastor, preacher, advocate and leader,
> — Joy Douglas Strome, Retired Pastor,
> Lake View Presbyterian Church, Chicago

Here is the story of one woman's heroic spiritual journey (my words—she would never describe herself this way), a woman who has loved, suffered, and served around the world. It is a story of a love for truth, a love for God and all God's children, a love for Creation, a commitment to justice and non-violence, and courage that has repeatedly pushed her to transcend her own comfort zones. She is, as her name suggests, a person of extreme *grace*, firmly rooted in the grace of God. But she is also a person of fierce commitment to transforming the world, especially her own nation, from centers of self-interest to centers of peace, wisdom, and justice. Read her story and be inspired to live your own story more faithfully!

> — The Rev. Dr. Richard L. "Dick" Hamm,
> Former General Minister and President of the Christian
> Church (Disciples of Christ) in the U.S. and Canada

In 1977, Tom Gyori encouraged me to work with the K'ekchi Indians near Lake Izabal, in Guatemala. Both he and his wife Grace were always helpful in supporting me during the beginning of this ministry. I praise God that God used them to encourage me in investing part of my life here for God.

> — Jose Luis Saguil,
> Presbyterian colleague and close friend in Guatemala.

A *Subversive* SEED-SAVER AND SOWER

a memoir

GRACE GYORI

ONEEARTH PUBLISHING
San Diego, California

A Subversive Seed-Saver and Sower: A Memoir
© 2022, Grace Gyori. All rights reserved.

Published by OneEarth Publishing, San Diego, California
TheOneEarthProject.com

ISBN 978-1-7340299-3-2 (paperback)
ISBN 978-1-7340299-4-9 (eBook)

Publication managed by AuthorImprints.com

I dedicate this book to my four children,
Tom Jr., Ken, Sonja and Jim.
All are life-affirming and life-giving individuals.

Inside

An Invitation

Y ou hold in your hands an invitation.

This invitation beckons you into a lovely garden of remembrances. Here you will find rich old growth, standing tall, protecting and nurturing innumerable stands of saplings. These in turn hover lovingly over young sprouts that keep multiplying every year. What a glorious display of God's abundant life and creation! Here you will find familiar and surprising examples of diversity of color, size, and even origin. You, my grandchildren, will eventually discover your own, beautiful self, displaying your unique contours and colors.

Grace Gyori

Foreword

Some write memoirs to justify their lives. Grace Gyori has written a memoir that reveals more of her life.

Initially she entitled her memoir, "A Subversive Seed-Saver." Indeed, she describes her love for spouting seeds and tending them all the way to harvest ... and then to save seeds and do it again next year. Seed-saver is also an apt metaphor for her life. Then, as I read it, I was so struck by how she not only has saved seeds but has sown them. ...everywhere she's gone. She has especially sown seeds that were subversive to systems of injustice and death.

Reflecting on the chapters of her life, they came to cluster for me into four periods:

(1) Her birth in China and living as the daughter of missionaries. Her years of childhood and education include a narrow escape from China when Japan invaded. Many of us reading her story will find these adventures unusual for childhood and years of education.

(2) For me, the second period begins when she meets and marries Chicagoan Tom Gyori. Together, they discerned God's call to be missionaries. This took them to

Guatemala with the Presbyterian Church USA. While there, Grace was into being a mother to four children and made sure of their education. All the while she herself was being radicalized by her experiences of the errors and destructions of US policies in supporting corrupt, Latin American authoritarian leaders. Why would her country do this? As she discovered, because the U.S. did not want any more Communist or Marxist governments in Latin America like Cuba had become.

(3) The end of missionary work in Guatemala brought them back to Chicago. Children were grown and gone. Tom was immediately engaged to serve Hispanic congregations in Chicago. But for Grace, there was no work. She'd saved a lot of subversive seeds during her missionary years, but now had nowhere to sow them. That changed dramatically when she met up with other religious groups who were taking groups to Guatemala and Latin America. Grace was just who they needed to be translator. In addition to translating, she was an interpreter for the people participating in these short immersions, so that they would understand the realities of what they were seeing. With the life she'd lived to date, and her skills in communicating what was happening, she sparkled in this work. The subversive seed saver was sowing them in the soils of peoples' minds and hearts.

(4) Time came for her and Tom to move out of Chicago and to their lakeshore home, the first home they'd ever purchased. Gradually, her life was shifting into a slower gear, but far from becoming inactive. A dozen years

later, she and Tom needed to shift down another gear. They were invited by Sonja and Ray Helmuth, daughter and son-in-law, just outside of Indianapolis, to live with them. Ray and Sonja promptly built an addition to their home to accommodate this change. From their new address, visits with family and friends filled their lives, whether going to see them or vice versa. Gardening and seed-saving continued in the side yard there and so did subversive seed sowing in all her interactions. This memoir surely sows subversive seeds into our minds and hearts as we read her amazing story.

A few years ago Grace obliged me when I asked to interview her for the Simpler OneEarth Podcast that a colleague and I were creating monthly. I was especially interested in highlighting the contrast in the two types of missionary work that had marked her life. The China Inland Mission (now Oversees Missionary Fellowship International) is about evangelization, church planting, reaching unreached people with Christianity. To my knowledge that style of missionary work has not come to terms with how Western it is. Furthermore, it is imperialistic in that it colonizes people into a worldview that forces them to deny the values and wisdom of their own culture, the culture that holds their identity.

By contrast, Grace and Tom's missionary work in Guatemala was totally different. There they accompanied and served local leadership. Decisions were made by the local people. Tom and Grace contributed to this decolonization of Christian faith which has too often been delivered in the garb of Western culture, whether Catholic or Protestant.

Grace was well into the third of the four periods of her story when I first saw her. I was attending a luncheon of the Chicago Religious Leaders Network for Latin America when a person I didn't know was being awarded for excellent work in human rights for Latin Americans. To receive this award, Grace Gyori was called forward. The moment left an impact on me.

Some months later, Juanita and I began attending a group of people whose minds and hearts had been radicalized by the witness and suffering of the people of Latin America. Juanita had gone on a two week immersion to Nicaragua and Guatemala, and needed this kind of group to process all the overwhelming feelings which demanded changes in her life. I had my own experiences for needing this kind of group. There, our relationship with Grace and Tom deepened. Through them we came to read *The Biblical Jubilee and the Struggle for Life*, written by their friends Ross and Gloria Kinsler. Reading and discussing this book with them and a few others led us in 1999 to form a nonprofit called Jubilee Economics Ministries. Gloria had led the two week immersion that was so infused by holy Presence among the people of Latin America that Juanita started on a different path—a path that continues to this day. And Grace has been a constant friend during all this unsettling, important transition.

When this memoir was first being conceived, Grace intended to write her story for friends and her family—a considerable audience in itself with marriages of grandchildren and then their families. But seed-saver and sower that she is, we now have for our reading a volume that is much more. As we read, we feel the pulse of God's subversive Spirit in so many of her adventures. And that Spirit mysteriously leaves the page and enters us. Many reading this memoir will experience some changes stirring in themselves.

This book can show readers the way to go for a life that is far more interested in justice than money. It can show the difference between activism and spiritual activism. It casts aside the notion that we need heroes and high profile people in order for change to happen. It shows us, instead, the transforming power of change through ordinary people, who are willing to trust God's Call to them (for that Call does come to all of us many, many times during our lives). It is in hearing and heading that Call that Grace offers us an extraordinary life; yet, reading carefully, we recognize an amazingly ordinary woman.

She eschewed patriarchy and hierarchies, believing that relationships with mutual respect were stronger and more loving. She saw through the systems designed by human egos that aim to give power and wealth to the people near society's top. She, instead, has trusted eco-systems for real power and wealth. Her life is a counter story to the American Dream. She was not seduced by it. Instead, the dream of Earth has lived in her ever more deeply over the years. Her eyes saw through many of the "gospels" that said we could trust our soul to find its joy in more things, more money, or more travel. Rather, she saw that these false gospels tragically disconnected people from the wealth in our souls—a tragedy now devastating our planet and destroying life itself. Grace has yearned for the wealth of a soul inhabited by the Divine. Toward that end she has saved and sown the seeds that subvert the thinking of this world and that lead us, amid our ego-designed systems, to our Creator.

Lee Van Ham
July 2022

Introduction

Little can be as rewarding as saving seeds. As Joan Chittister said in a recent book, "We are here to seed the present with godliness so that others may someday reap the best of what we sowed." Being bearers of the seeds of God's love is a life-fulfilling vocation. This is an invitation to share my "treasure house of fertile seeds", of life experiences, feelings and learnings gained over the expanse of 88 years living in this abundant garden called God's Good Earth. So many of these memories are shaped and emboldened by the Psalms.

As a Master Gardener, I have been saving seeds from earlier harvests to use in starting a new garden every spring. As to the "subversive" part, many of you know me as a non-conformist, sometimes a willing risk taker, and not confined to following a particular recipe, while cooking, for example. That I refuse to plant genetically modified seeds in our garden, is another example of my subversive bent.

The marriage of Elizabeth and Julius Gyori produced the productive seedling of Thomas William, their only child, born on December 5, 1931. Tom later became my beloved husband, and we produced four children. In turn, their progeny numbered ten between them. Now, I am the proud great grandmother of eleven, new, little people, each promising hope and renewal in this broken world of ours.

CHAPTER 1

My Memoir Begins in China

LYDIA ASPINAL ALLEN

Unflinching, determined, courageous,
single, female, assured of her call,
Lydia sailed from Australia in the mid 1800s.

She obeyed God's beckoning her to China.

There, she married Henry Albert Churchill Allen
in Kunming, Yunnan,
Becoming the undisputed matriarch of the Allen family.

— Lydia Aspinal Allen was my grandmother.

MABEL GERALDINE KINNEY ALLEN

Adventuresome, dedicated and competent,
Mabel left the comforts of rural Ludington, Michigan,
worked her way through Moody Bible Institute
in urban Chicago, in 1926,
preparing to follow God's call to China.

Oct. 11, 1928, she boarded the "Empress of Asia"
to begin her life as a missionary in China.

She, too, began her new life in Kunming.

— Mabel Geraldine Kinney Allen was my mother.

T he China Inland Mission, CIM, a British mission board, was the organization my grandfather, H. A. C. Allen, joined in his native England. He preceded Lydia, his wife, to China and was among the founders of the inland outpost of the CIM in Kunming, Yunnan. This province is in a beautiful, mountainous southwest corner of China, bordering on "Burma Road". Grandpa became a recognized missionary statesman by all who worked with him. Lydia was probably credited more for "humbly, obediently subjugating herself to 'God's call,'" than for her actual strength of character and courage.

My father was born in Kunming, and in accord with the mission policy, at the age of five was sent to the mission school in Chefoo, situated in the northeast of China on the Pacific coast. He received the equivalent of K-12 schooling there. Since the CIM granted one year of furlough after eight years of service it may well be that Daddy didn't see his parents for eight years running. Upon completion of his studies in Chefoo, he travelled to the U.S. where he continued further studies in three different Bible Schools. Knowing no other life than that of China, he returned as a missionary with the CIM, rejoining his parents in Kunming, where he met my mom. After she had finished language school, they were married on April 17, 1930, in Kunming.

On January 8, 1934, I, Grace Irene, was born to Arthur and Mabel Allen in Kunming, I joined Geraldine, an older sister by three years. My first five years were lived with my family in Tonghai, not far from Kunming. Tragically, Geraldine died at the age of five in Daddy's arms as he was on his way to seek medical help for her combination of diphtheria and whooping cough. In 1939, my sister Rosaline was born, completing our family.

Following in my father's footsteps, when I reached the age of five, I left for school in Chefoo. My mother accompanied me as far as Hong Kong. In that port city, she entrusted me to the care of another missionary woman to take me and David Michelle to school. David wrote later that upon arriving in Chefoo, he held my hand and obstinately refused to mount the steps to the school, an unsuccessful attempt at rebellion by a five year old.

My eighteen months in Chefoo were happy and gave me a good educational foundation in the British school system. During that time, 1939 through 1941, war clouds were looming. Japan had already invaded areas around Chefoo when my parents' furlough became due. They went north to pick me up to take me with them to Michigan, where they planned to spend the next year. Surely, they knew what was going on between Japan and China. I never asked. We left Chefoo without incident and sailed down to Shanghai. As they were preparing our papers for leaving, it became evident that I did not have a visa for the U.S.

I was a British citizen like my dad. For some reason I was not included on his visa. My parents saw no other option than to leave me behind under the care of other missionaries, hoping that a visa would be granted before the next ship left bound for the U.S., Mom took me out for an ice cream cone the evening before their ship was to leave. Providentially, during the night some U.S. military personnel received a short-wave message from the States, granting visas to two children, and I was one of them! Daddy and I scurried around Shanghai the next morning gathering papers and signatures needed for me to successfully join them on the ship departing that day. It turned out that only one more passenger ship, the Gripsholm, left Shanghai for the U.S., shortly before Japan bombed Pearl Harbor on December 7. This resulted in our declaration of war with Japan. Soon all expatriates living in Chefoo were interned in a Japanese concentration camp, housed in a former Presbyterian mission compound not too far inland. Several of my first cousins, David Michelle, and my future stepmother were all interned there. There but for the grace of God, I would have gone, too!

CHAPTER 2

Furlough 1942 in Michigan

Adonai, show me the path I should tread...
Let your nurturing Spirit guide me
On a safe and level path.

PSALM 149:8,10,

After disembarking in San Francisco, Mom wanted to take advantage of this opportunity to explore some important sites in our beautiful country. As the four of us made our way across the U.S. by train, we stopped at the Grand Canyon, marveling at its grandeur. We finally arrived in Ludington, Michigan, my mom's hometown. There we were met by my Uncle Welland Kinney. Rosaline and I rode in the back of Uncle Welland's pick up with our cousins Elwyn and Lavonne. In my attempt to break the silence, I asked them, "Have you forgotten your Chinese?" Clearly, I was unaware that such a question made little sense to them, but was uppermost on my mind. They were a bit nonplussed, no doubt!

Our first home was in the second-floor apartment of the Frederick's farmhouse, which didn't have indoor plumbing. I well remember our Saturday evening baths in a round, tin bathtub, brought inside the kitchen. This house was located down the hill from Aunt Margarite and Uncle Emery's farm on U.S. 31. Rosaline and I had a mile's walk to the local one-room schoolhouse. Those daily walks—come rain, snow, or shine are memorable because I always took the lead, and I became impatient with Rosaline as she lagged behind. We attended this school only one year, as I recall.

Soon, Daddy accepted a call to serve as the pastor of a small, rural Methodist parish not far away. He served three churches, and we lived in Crystal Valley. My happy memories of the next three years living there are filled with fun, as Rosaline and I explored the woods behind our home, imagining encounters with Indians, and other interesting people. Our home was comfortable but rudimentary, with electricity, no indoor plumbing, except for a hand pump by the kitchen sink. We cooked on a wood burning range.

Mother had a large garden in which this subversive seed saver was planted. Little would I have guessed how long those seeds would lie dormant. They sprouted timidly in a roof top garden in Guatemala City years later. It was not until some fifty years later, however, when I received my official title of "Master Gardener" from the University of Illinois that those early seeds finally produced. Then they reproduced bountifully in the "Organic Faith Community Garden" that Tom and I initiated at Ravenswood Presbyterian Church in Chicago. Although not bearing that name any longer, it is still growing lovely edibles in the same spot, now being managed by the Montessori School housed in the church.

Back in Crystal Valley, the local, one-room grade school was just around the corner from our house, with Miss Maisie as the teacher. While living in Crystal Valley, Daddy taught both of us how to swim. Swimming had been a passion of his while living on the Pacific coast of China in Chefoo. Vacations in northern Michigan were also memorable family times.

More happy years followed after Daddy left the pastorate and began working in the Dow Chemical Plant in Ludington, Michigan. We moved into a house on one of my Uncle Emery's farms, near Ludington. Every time we moved, Rosaline and I would look for the best trees to climb in the vicinity. Here, we had a perfect one from which we could practice tricks and climb at will. Daddy bought us a "modern" two wheel bike for our transportation to school, at least a mile away from home. I carried Rosaline on the bike, sitting in front of me. Soon after receiving this new bike, I crashed it, denting the lovely bike, and making me feel terrible! Marchido Grade School was another one-room school, where our Aunt Francis Kinney was our teacher and our cousins Lavonne and Elwin were also students. From there I graduated from the eighth grade.

Mom and Dad had reapplied to the China Inland Mission, hoping to return to China. Surprisingly, they were informed that their application was rejected because of an accusation the mission board had received that Daddy was not 'orthodox enough'! Upon investigating, it was discovered that a neighboring pastor had informed them that Daddy failed to issue an "invitation" calling people forward to accept Christ as Savior, during a funeral he had conducted. Mom and Daddy were very disturbed by this, of course, and Mom pursued the issue until they were finally accepted. Their return was scheduled for the late summer of 1947.

CHAPTER 3

Transition Time Again

*I will teach you and show you the
   way you should walk;
I will counsel you, and keep watch over you.*
                                    PSALM 32:8

M y future became an issue again, as I was ready to begin high school. Feeling keenly that we should receive a Christian education, my parents enrolled me in Wheaton College Academy, outside of Wheaton, Illinois. I unquestioningly went along with their decision to have me live in Wheaton during the school year and spend summer vacations with Aunt Francis and Uncle Welland Kinney, near Ludington, on their farm. Living with them and my two cousins, time was pleasantly spent helping out with the routine chores of country living. This included picking fruit as it matured, helping with Aunt Francis's garden and riding their pony, Prince. One summer they encouraged me to learn to drive their recently purchased black Chevrolet sedan. It was parked under some trees in the yard, and I promptly drove into one, smashing the front of the car. That ended my meagre attempts to learn to drive! Later, after marrying Tom, he tried to teach me, but each time he did, I became pregnant! After four deliveries, I decided, enough was enough! Hence, I never again even tried to drive a car! I often said I had produced four chauffeurs, so what was the need?

My sister Rosaline accompanied my parents back to China and was enrolled in the Chefoo School, which had been relocated to Kuling, in central China, atop a mountain in a lush, resort area. She was never happy there, feeling very much an outsider all four years. She spent one vacation with our parents, in Tunghai, which was the only time she saw them during her 4 years of school in China. How aware were our parents about how that experience traumatized her?

In 1950, when the Communist regime took power in China, most foreigners were evicted, including our family. Daddy wrote: "When the Communists took over Yunnan, and finally moved into our home in Tonghai, as guests, Mabel (my mother) rose to the occasion. She was so casual about their presence that they picked up their guns after one week's residence and never returned."

In the meantime, Rosaline was evacuated with the entire Chefoo school and she returned to the U.S. accompanied by a missionary woman, Mrs. Crapuchettes. I was a high school senior at Wheaton Academy at the time. When I learned of Rosaline's planned arrival at Chicago's Union Station, I wondered how I would recognize this sister whom I had not seen in four years? Indeed, she presented a rather sorry sight, walking forlornly beside the train, wearing a beige wool coat and a scarf covering her head. She looked like a poor, lost refugee to me! I took her with me to Wheaton Academy. After a few days, I put her on a bus to Ludington, where she was to stay with

Aunt Marguerite and Uncle Emery Kinney near Ludington, awaiting our parents' return.

Mother was the next to leave China. She and my Aunt Lucille Allen travelled together, separating upon reaching the States. My aunt, wife of Daddy's brother Will, returned to her home in Washington state, while Mother made her way back to hers in Michigan by way of a stop in Chicago. I knew when Mom had arrived when I saw her Bible on the dresser in my apartment in Oak Park, where I lived for the summer after graduating from high school. A classmate and I were working as nurses' aides in West Suburban Hospital. I had not known my parents' itineraries before they arrived, so I sent welcoming flowers to Mom somewhere on the East Coast, only to learn too late, that she had crossed the Pacific!

Meanwhile, Daddy and Uncle Will flew from Hong Kong to Australia, where Uncle Will had previously studied and where some cousins lived. Then he went on to England to visit 93-year-old Grandpa Allen, and other relatives before returning to the U.S. Finally, Daddy was reunited with my mom and Rosaline in Ludington.

While my family was dealing with the growing turmoil in China, and their unexpected evacuation, I was enjoying my four years at Wheaton Academy. Memories which stand out include the joy of singing in the Academy Glee Club, working in the school's dining room, a happy summer vacation spent with classmate Mary Lou Rodgers in her home in Arkansas and other ordinary high school activities.

Upon graduating and after my summer working in Oak Park in the hospital, I returned to Michigan to join my family as we all reunited in Highland Park, Michigan. My Aunt

Irene Tuggy had invited my parents to move in with her in Highland Park and care for her in exchange for rent, which they did. Mom cared for Aunt Irene until she died. We inherited the property. I worked in an office in downtown Detroit for the summer of 1951. Rosaline was enrolled in a Christian boarding high school in Spring Arbor, Michigan, where she began that fall.

I enrolled in the nursing program of Wheaton College, housed in West Suburban Hospital in Oak Park, Illinois. My memories of nurses' training are pleasant but uneventful. I was disappointed in not being selected to take my pediatrics rotation at the Children's Hospital in Chicago; instead stayed at West Suburban. Moving into my own room my senior year was a big deal for me, living a bit more independently across the street from the hospital.

> *Seeds of self-sufficiency, inadvertently planted*
> *upon departing Tunghai so long ago,*
> *were nurtured, fertilized, and watered*
> *during my years with family in Michigan.*
>
> *After seven years of Wheaton College grafting,*
> *this sapling of Grace Irene Allen*
> *needed fresh sunlight, wind and rain*
> *for her to grow into maturity.*
>
> *The strength of her boughs*
> *needed the environs of a different climate*
> *which she sought tentatively*
> *in the landscape of the University of Illinois.*

This was a fortuitous move. I became active in Inter Varsity Christian Fellowship where I met Tom Gyori, the president of IVCF at the time. Our courtship was both rich and frugal. Tom, who had grown up in a non-religious home, had been converted to Christianity during high school in Chicago, at a Youth For Christ rally. After that he became involved in the Buena Memorial Presbyterian Church in Chicago, where several of his classmates were members. Therefore, he was not straddled by the religious rules which had governed my faith expressions and understandings. I credit him for the beginning of the broadening of my faith.

Our dating began with taking mid-morning coffee breaks. As we became better acquainted, it soon became clear that we were indeed falling in love with each other. Our dates were limited both by meager finances, and by busy school schedules and activities. Undeterred, our relationship flourished, and soon I was introduced to his family in Chicago.

I lived in a small co-op house in Champaign, which was an early experience of 'alternative' living options. Helen Marten, my roommate, became a life-long friend.

CHAPTER 4

A Harvest of Love

The fertile seeds of friendship
found a home in fertile hearts.

With careful nurturing
they germinated into love.

Fertilized with frequent contacts
sprouting appeared above the surface
of everyday campus life.

Roots penetrated prepared soil.

Meeting respective parents
proved welcoming and accepting.

Growing was interrupted by Tom's hepatitis
where Grace demonstrated caring.

Finally, engagement established maturation
and fondness was expressed in love.

Plans for a fall wedding
developed the buds about to bloom.

A happy honeymoon in Wisconsin
showed the beauty of love in gorgeous blossom.

Fruit born from the flowers
came to maturity with Tommy's birth
and full harvest came later with Ken, Sonja, and Jim

> **This is the day our God has made—**
> **let us celebrate with joy!**
>
> **PSALM 118:24**

Sixty-five years ago, our wedding day dawned, filled with sunshine, anxiety, anticipation and exquisite joy. With unquestioning confidence in a loving God, who had brought us to this place, Tom and I celebrated every moment of this signature day. Surrounded by our families and closest friends, we felt beloved. Tom's home church was the unquestioned site for this life-giving event.

The Buena Memorial Presbyterian Church was a beautiful Gothic structure adorned with gorgeous stained-glass windows. But the center aisle was so, so long! Maxine Ramseyer, wife of Tom's best friend, was our organist, and Marie Crapuchettes sang. Each of us had invited three people to serve as our attendants, with Rosaline as my maid of honor and John Vaughn as Tom's best man. Rev. Dr. David Noble, the pastor, officiated in a very traditional ceremony. We left the wedding in style, in a fancy yellow convertible!

Fortunately, our many friends were more than generous in gifting us with the basics we needed to begin our married life. These were beautifully displayed at our reception in the church basement following our lovely wedding. Tom bought his first car prior to our wedding, and it proudly transported us on our honeymoon. He had dreamed of taking his bride to the cottages on a small lake in northern Wisconsin, where he and his family had spent some memorable vacations. Since the tourist season was over, we found ourselves ensconced in a simple little cottage, peacefully enjoying our few days in privacy and happiness.

We had taken the electric fry pan, a wedding gift, and I enjoyed the challenges of cooking in it. One afternoon, we scavenged a harvested potato field and enjoyed delicious new potatoes for dinner that evening. Some friends of Tom's, owned property around a private lake nearby, where we went skinny dipping, which was exciting! All too soon we had to head back south, pick up our few earthly belongings and wend our way to Louisville, Kentucky, where Tom had enrolled in the Presbyterian Seminary.

CHAPTER 5

Preparing for Service

Whether or not we would be missionaries was at this point an open question for us, not a certainty. But we did know that we were called to lives of service. So we prepared. First, Tom went to seminary in Louisville, Kentucky, and I found a job as a nurse in hospital. Then, as Tom was being ordained in Chicago, I missed it. But for a joyful reason. I I was in the hospital giving birth to Kenneth Allen, our second son. Tom soon took a position as assistant pastor in Mt. Prospect, Illinois, a congregation where I also worked in Christian Education.

By now, becoming missionaries was clearer in our hearts, so we enrolled in the Stony Point Conference Center in New York where missionaries were trained in theology and cultures. It was the best educational community and experience we'd had. Soon we were off to Central America to learn a new language and move into service.

Louisville, Kentucky

> *Educate me, Adonai, in the way of your statutes,*
>   *And I will keep them to the end.*
> *Give me discernment, that I may observe your law*
>   *And obey it with all my heart.*
>   **PSALM 119:33**

The "fertile crescent" apartments on campus were all occupied, so we had to find our own apartment. We found an
upstairs, efficiency apartment near-by and moved into our
first home. Tom still had some benefits from the G.I. bill, as
he was a Korean War veteran. That gave us a little financial
cushion to begin our married life, which helped until I found
employment in the Baptist Hospital, where I worked nights in
the surgical department. Soon we made friends among other
seminary couples, among them Jack and Emily Stull. She was
also a nurse and later helped me find work teaching nursing
students at the same hospital. She already had a baby, so when
our son Tom was born, on January 30, 1959, she offered to care
for him so I could work, which suited us all. I remember a particular financially lean period after we had moved into a larger
space, when we had to break Tom's glass brick bank in which
he had been saving pennies for years. We took the money to a
bank in exchange for dollars, to see us through.

The day my labor started before Tom Jr. was born, I felt
infused with incredible energy and spent the day house clean-
ing, washing windows, and putting everything in order to
welcome him. My Mom came to help me after his delivery
and proved to be a patient presence. One day I asked her why

she seemed so reluctant to pick him up. She told me how her mother-in-law had been so critical of her and the ways she handled Rosaline and me when we were born, that Mom didn't want to appear to be interfering inordinately in baby Tommy's care!

While still living in Louisville, we visited my folks, who were then living and working near Asheville, North Carolina, at Ben Lippen Academy, a Christian boarding high school. I was displeased with the fact that they were assigned as dorm parents, living in one of the dorms. I felt they were way too qualified to fulfill the demeaning tasks given them. Also, l was feeling a bit rebellious, resisting my parents' expectations of openly reading my Bible and praying when they wanted me to. Upon our return home, Mom wrote a letter to me stating how much they had enjoyed hosting us and especially two-year-old Tommy. However, she lamented my "loss of faith". This comment hurt me deeply, eliciting a detailed response, defending my faith practices. I'm sorry I did not keep those letters, as they had touched a deep chord within.

As Tom neared the end of his seminary education, we did a lot of discerning about where God might be calling us to serve. Because of my ambivalent feelings about missionary work, that was not my first choice! However, we finally agreed to keep that door open. In the meantime, Tom needed a job. I was in the third trimester of my second pregnancy. As we sent in our application to the Presbyterian mission agency, the Commission on Ecumenical Mission and Relations (COEMAR), Tom looked for other openings. A high school friend of Tom's, Conway Ramseyer, an ordained clergy in Chicago, suggested Tom apply for an opening in the Mt. Prospect Presbyterian

Church. This was a vibrant, growing congregation pastored by another former member of Buena Presbyterian Church, Rev. Norm Herbert, who was looking for an assistant. Tom applied and was called to work with him.

Mt. Prospect, Illinois

On June 20, 1960, the day before Tom's ordination, our son Ken decided to make his appearance in the Swedish Covenant Hospital in Chicago. Hospital policy would not allow me to be dismissed to attend this seminal event. My sister Rosaline went in my stead and was mistaken for Tom's wife.

Our three years with the Mt. Prospect church turned out to be a time of new learnings for me, especially regarding new approaches to Christian Education. I was introduced to the concept of learning centers around the classroom, instead of teaching children only while seated in rows. Some of these new ideas influenced my future work in education.

Not only new learnings were taking place, but new adventures as well. We were considered rather foolhardy, by my Aunt Frances in Ludington, Michigan. We took three-month-old Kenny and Tommy, now a robust year and a half, up there to visit. Instead of staying with my aunt and uncle, we put up our tent, in the Ludington State Park camp grounds. Aunt Frances believed it neither healthy or proper to subject baby Kenny to such sandy privations!

When Ken was about 18 months old, Tom and I took Tommy with us on a vacation in the boundary waters of northern Minnesota. How we enjoyed canoeing, fishing, and camping while there. One afternoon while boating across a lake, the motor fell off the boat, and sank to the bottom. Nothing to do but to pick up the oars and row back to shore. We had left Kenny with Grandma and Grandpa Gyori in Chicago. He took his first steps while with them!

Back in Mt. Prospect, we continued to pursue missionary service and were offered several options in different countries, over a period of three years. Finally, Rev. John Sinclair, then secretary for Latin America, came calling. He was convinced that we should serve in Latin America where there were calls for a couple with our skills, a clergyperson and a nurse. When I told him I was three months pregnant, he waved that information aside. We agreed to pursue these options and made our way to the Missionary Orientation Center in Stony Point, New York.

New York
Stony Point Missionary Orientation Center

> *Serve our God with gladness!*
> *Enter into God's presence with a joyful song!*
> *Know that Adonai is God!*
> *Our God made us, and we belong to the Creator;*
>   *We are God's people*
>   *And the sheep of God's pasture.*
>   **PSALM 100:1–3**

The next six months became the richest and most thorough educational experiences either of us had ever known! These were shared with at least fifty other aspiring missionaries from four or five other denominations, and we were all destined for the four corners of the globe. We lived together with our respective spouses and families on a beautiful campus, sharing meals, field trips and entertainment, as well as lectures and intensive studies in theology and world cultures. We also discussed practical issues of living outside of the U.S. During this memorable time, we established deep, life-long friendships, some of which we enjoy to this day. Near completion of our time there, determinations were made concerning final acceptance by the Presbyterian Commission on Ecumenical Mission and Relations (COEMAR) and our placement of service. For us the choice was between serving in Chile, or Guatemala. Fortunately for us, the latter won.

Sonja Elizabeth was born on March 25, 1962, in Suffern, New York. As excited as we were to welcome a lovely daughter into our family, she was not a happy baby and seemed to cry for the first year of her life! Caring for baby Sonja did crimp my style a bit regarding participation in all the activities at Stony Point. The Center was well equipped to care for our growing families, with competent childcare for all the offspring.

We who were Presbyterians were commissioned in New York City upon completion of our studies at Stony Point. Following that much anticipated event, we were enrolled in an intensive course in linguistics on the campus of Drew University in New Jersey. These studies proved to be much less meaningful or helpful to me as I was fully engaged with caring for our three young children.

CHAPTER 6

Costa Rica

Memory blurs regarding what transpired in the weeks between leaving Drew University and preparing to leave the U.S. for language school in San Jose, Costa Rica, We fulfilled our plans to make a stop-over in Guatemala. We were welcomed into the Presbyterian guest apartment for a couple of days. Our discomfort in not speaking Spanish came to the fore when we shopped in the local supermarket for basic food items. Trusting the clerks at the check-out was easier than the embarrassment of not even understanding the currency.

In San Jose we were enrolled in the ecumenical language institute, joining aspiring missionaries assigned to work throughout Latin America, The students represented a wide variety of denominational sending bodies, which turned out to be quite a challenge in and of itself. A wide variety of differing theological positions were discussed, even argued about in some of the language classes.

We had been assigned to living accommodations in a gated community, where we had the comfort of an apartment with several bedrooms, enough to comfortably house our young family. Our classes were held in the mornings, leaving the afternoons for study and care for our household tasks. Neither Tom nor l proved to be particularly adept at language learning, but after this immersion in the Spanish language, even we became at least functional in understanding and speaking it. While in San Jose, we bought a VW minivan which we drove to Guatemala upon finishing our language studies. Since these were pre-seat belt days, our three children roamed freely over the packed back of the vehicle, enjoying one of the many long drives we took as a family over the course of the upcoming years.

CHAPTER 7

Guatemala

One of the first ingenious things Tom arranged for us upon our arrival in Guatemala City, was a tour of each of our Presbyterian mission stations across the country. Tom's people skills shone! Upon meeting each missionary serving the Guatemalan Presbyterian Church, we became acquainted early on with our faithful, talented, and creative colleagues. That tour served us well as a foundational preparation, helping us to understand the scope of the vision and mission of the work in which we would be engaged. Our first stop was in San Felipe, Retaluleu, where our seminary had recently been relocated from the capital. We were hosted by Vera and Charles Ainley, senior missionaries, who were accompanying the church through a historic shift in theological education. Ralph Winters, another missionary, was developing the vision of theological education by extension, which became known internationally as TEE. Along with Genette and Jim Emery, and later joined by Gloria and Ross Kinsler, they envisioned taking seminary training to local congregational leaders, rather than pulling students away from home to attend a school in an unfamiliar urban setting. Also, the students could continue in their local ministries maintaining their work and livelihoods. Professors went to them, even sometimes meeting under bridges!

We met Ruth Wardell, a nurse, and Ralph and Roberta Winters, all living and working in the Mam Center, in San Juan Ostuncalco, outside of Quetzaltenango, in the highlands. In each home, we enjoyed warm hospitality and learned so much about the people and work of the Presbyterian Church of Guatemala.

Among my first assignments upon moving to Guatemala City, was to accompany a Guatemalan physician in attending a rural medical clinic in El Rancho, located north of the capital. My lack of expertise in the language really hit home then, not understanding local sayings, and being embarrassed by not knowing what some simple terms meant, such as "pisto," for money. Fortunately, I muddled through without any major catastrophes!

Even more difficult was being "in charge" of a city clinic in the capital. There, Doctor Roberto Hernandez was the attending physician. A well-qualified Guatemalan nurse, with much more expertise and experience than I, was a colleague. How often I found myself leaving a consultation to ask her what in the world the doctor had prescribed for the patient! Years later, Dr. Hernandez spoke English to us, very clearly, and I was incensed that he had humiliated me so shamefully years before! Subsequently we became good friends.

El Progreso, Guastatoya

We were assigned to El Progreso, Guastatoya, the capital of the department by the same name. Here we moved into a

very comfortable home, built around a large patio, containing a mango, jocote, and lemon trees. What an ideal setting
where three young children could thrive! There, I planted
my first garden, only to discover I could not even grow swiss
chard, which is among the least difficult and most prolific of
vegetables. However, our foot long green beans flourished
beautifully.

One of my most fulfilling adventures took place in our
converted chicken coup, in the far corner of the patio. There,
for three years I taught Tommy and Kenny. It was so much
fun for me, using the Calvert Correspondence curriculum as a
guide. Most enjoyable, were the extras I tagged on! While we
were busy learning together, Sonja played happily, climbing
trees and just plain enjoying life.

While in El Progreso, our family's almost continual attraction to pets began. We acquired several cats, not more
than one at a time. One we considered mentally challenged.
He would prowl around the neighborhood every night and
return home battered and bruised. We had a lovely German
Shepherd named Scamp. She became pregnant and delivered
a litter during a visit by Tom's parents. We set up chairs surrounding the "birthing box" we had set up for her. That we
would expose our children to such an event surprised our
good friend, Samuel Mejia. I'm sure there were many other
"strange" behaviors these gringos did, which appalled many!

Tom had been assigned to work in the North Presbytery,
which was the reason for our move to El Progreso. We were
the first missionaries to live there, and the leaders weren't
quite sure what to do with Tom. His predecessors had driven
there from the capital with their sound equipment mounted

on a truck and providing movies and music to the churches, as well as sermons. Soon Tom became involved with the Theological Education by Extension program, some community development work, and fulfilling tasks assigned by the presbytery. Eventually, he worked with others in developing the Icthus program for junior high and high school youth. This program has grown over the years, now encompassing all Latin America,

Shortly before our arrival in Guatemala, the National Presbyterian Church had sold the American Hospital, leaving the sale money to the Synod to use for medical programming. I was invited to help envision such an enterprise. I had read about the Chinese barefoot doctors and other alternative training programs for lay medical practitioners. Together with Dr. Annette Fortin, we developed a health promoter program for Indigenous men chosen by their communities to learn basic health procedures including basic diagnosis, and treatments for common disorders. The major requirement for participation, aside from being chosen locally, was that they be able to read and write Spanish as the materials were written in that language. The program was developed among the Mam Indians in the Mam Clinic, in San Juan, Ostuncalco, outside of Quetzaltenango. That was a long way from El Progreso, so I was not involved in the day-to-day teaching of the curriculum. This kind of medical training is now quite common throughout Latin America.

Our Children

> *Children are the heritage God gives us;*
> *Our descendants are our rewards.*
> **PSALM 127:3**

James Arthur, conceived in El Progreso, was born in Guatemala City on August 25, 1965. Jimmy completed our family and was a happy, loving little one, enjoyed by one and all. Having an infant in our family didn't seem to deter us from our school routine.

As a family we enjoyed many day trips around the country. A favorite was to Pasa Bien, a delightful place where we hiked, picnicked, and swam in the cold, shallow waters of a mountain stream which tumbled through rocks with a low waterfall nearby. Also, the mission had two lake houses each on the shores of lovely lakes: Lake Amatitlan, just outside of Guatemala City, and Lake Atitlan near Panajachel. This one we named Ruchichoy where many happy days of vacation were enjoyed by each of the missionary families. Also, it was the gathering place for annual mission meetings.

Lake Atitlan is the crown jewel of Guatemala, surrounded by picturesque domed volcanoes and crystal-clear water, due to the incredible depth of the lake. The shoreline came right up to the low wall bordering the Ruchichoy property, making private access to the water easy for all of us. Upon revisiting Atitlan recently, I discovered that the lake had receded at least two blocks from the boundaries we had enjoyed. allowing construction of houses and streets into what had been the sandy bottom of the lake. Also, the water has become so polluted, that fisher people complain of both the reduced size and scarcity of fish, endangering their livelihoods as well as their diets. We were told that the very life of the lake may be limited to less than ten years from now.

What fun it is to now listen to our children recount some of their adventures to their respective children! Jim recently recalled the evening when he and a neighbor buddy had decided to build an obstacle bike course in a field near our house in Guatemala City. Unfortunately, it was adjacent to a local well-guarded power plant. To add to the drama, it was getting dark when they were beginning to trace the course they had planned. Before long, two policemen arrived and asked the boys just what they thought they were doing. Needless to say, the boys beat a hasty retreat!

Big brother Tom was always inventing great adventures for his siblings to do. One was to use umbrellas as parachutes, as he watched them jump off the roof.

Ken won't forget his anger at the bus driver who ran over his soccer ball as it passed our house in Zone 2. After memorizing the bus's number, Ken patiently waited for it to makes its return run down our street. Ken was waiting with a pail full of water to dump on the bus when it showed up. Unfortunately, his dad arrived just as the bus approached and Ken threw the water from the garage roof on Tom's head! Afraid of the consequences, Ken fled to hide under the covers of his bed. Hardly a wise hideout, as Tom quickly found him and after listening to Ken's story, laughter resonated through the house.

Not being the adventurous one, Sonja's story is one I remember. While we still lived in Guastatoya, she caught her finger in a door. A few days after initial first aid, her fingernail turned black, and the pressure became most painful. Nothing for it but take her to the hospital in Guatemala City and seek professional attention from Dr. Hernandez. I was not allowed to accompany her into the inner sanctum, so all I could hear were anguished cries as her fingernail was removed. Being only three or four, she was justifiably frightened by the strangely robed people and the even stranger environment of the hospital. It was years before she could forgive Dr. Hernandez, refusing to talk with him, even crossing the street if she saw him!

Mothering four delightful children has been the most humbling and fulfilling joy of my life. Growing and learning together for fifteen years in Guatemala was an exhilarating experience. My husband Tom and I were excited and challenged by their development from infancy through the teen years. Beautiful Guatemala provided us with a rich diversity of culture, language and valuable mentors as our lives intermingled with "Guatemaltecos."

The six of us learned together the values of curiosity and humor, generosity and sharing, compassion and forgiveness, courage and wisdom, humility and awe. The rewards of mothering never end. Two of our children are now grandparents giving me the honor of being a great grandmother ten times!

Like any family we encountered ups and downs, successes and failures. God is leading us into pardon and healing.

Today the Gyori clan embraces more than thirty remarkable human beings. The roots and branches of this family encircle the globe. From England, Australia, China, Hungary, Ukraine, Turkey, and Spain, to Brazil, Ecuador, Guatemala,

Mexico and Puerto Rico we have come together in the United States.

My family is my ode to joy!

CHAPTER 8

First Furlough

We chose to follow the five-year plan, five years in Guatemala followed by one year back home in the U.S. Our first furlough was in 1967–68. Tom chose to pursue a master's program in adult education at Michigan State University in East Lansing. My sister was living in Ann Arbor, and our colleagues, Ruth and John Hazelton, chose to live in the area as well. Other missionary friends from Guatemala, Genette and Jim Emery, were finishing their furlough there, when we arrived. Sonja and her two older brothers were enrolled in the local elementary school near the little house we rented. Because Tom was studying and my time was filled with mothering, we did not do the usual itineration, visiting supporting churches outside of a few in Michigan and Illinois.

One near mishap occurred when Tom and Ken became involved in starting a fire in a field near the school. Needless to say they were roundly reprimanded for those misdeeds by the "powers that be!"

My soul is weary with sorrow;
Strengthen me according to thy word.
                                    PSALM 119:28

My parents lived in Asheville, North Carolina, where my mom was held in the grips of Lou Gehrig's disease, or amyotrophic lateral sclerosis. Although wheelchair bound, she and Daddy came to visit us in East Lansing, for Christmas of 1967. After eating a corn soup I had made for lunch, some pepper irritated her throat and she began to cough, and was unable to stop. Finally, Tom and Daddy took her to the hospital where they were unable to control her coughing. She died before midnight. I was in shock and unable to rid myself of guilt for that fateful lunch. Fortunately, Rosaline lived nearby, so she joined us in grieving. We had a small funeral service in the local Presbyterian Church with our friend Jim Emery presiding. We then accompanied her body to Ludington, Michigan, across the state, to be buried beside her parents in a cemetery there.

I carry regrets that I didn't live with my parents the usual number of years due to our separation, they in China, and I in the U.S. Also, I long for Mom's answers to so many unanswered questions. Some of these queries I articulated in a piece I wrote after her death: "What were your thoughts, dreams, expectations as you crossed the Pacific, headed for life in unknown China?" "How was the re-entry into U.S. life and culture during your first furlough?" "What did telling and re-telling your China stories do to you?" "How did you feel bidding your 5 ½ year old daughter, Grace Irene, farewell in Hong Kong, leaving her in the care of another missionary woman to take her up the long coast to Chefoo School, knowing you would not see her for at least 18 months when your next furlough was due?" "What fears beset you as you made the painful decision to leave Grace behind in Shanghai in August 1941 because she lacked the proper visa to travel with you as you embarked for the U.S.?" "How profoundly relieved you had to have been when her permit was granted at the very last minute!" She was again confronted with the same decision about leaving me behind as they felt called to return to China, in 1947. That's when they enrolled me in Wheaton College Academy in Wheaton, Illinois, a Christian boarding high school. What went through her mind having to leave me yet again? They took sister Rosaline with them and left her in the CIM mission school now relocated in Kuling, in the center of the country. How concerned, or even aware was she of how Rosaline hated being there for four years, being able to see them only once during that time?

After Mom died, I wrote, "Ours was not an intimate family, having been separated so many times. Nevertheless, you continued to be the strong, dependable focal point of our family. You were a happy, rather private woman. At the same time, you were a gifted leader, especially in your local church. When you were employed in a bookstore, your pleasant personality and business acumen shone." It is hard to write about Mom's death especially with so many unanswered questions floating around.

Daddy also wrote movingly about their life together. "All we have and are come from His hand, and her work seemed to be just an extension of His hands of sympathy and compassion." He went on to tell of her being assigned to Kunming, the capital of Yunnan province. Their short courtship was followed by their marriage. About their last months in Tnghai, where they lived, he wrote: "New believers found the chapel and our home to be almost the center of their social life, so came each night of the week, not just Sundays. Mabel's smile and love never failed to strike a response in their hearts."

Back to our life in East Lansing, Michigan, during that year we made a number of trips to Chicago. Our purpose was to spend time with Tom's folks, where they accommodated us in their very limited one-bedroom garden apartment. Being the gracious, generous people they were, they made room for all six of us, in addition to themselves! Both Tom and I felt the importance of taking as much advantage as possible to help our children to know and interact with their grandparents. Fortunately, all four of our parents visited us several times in Guatemala. During our furloughs, we always made a conscious effort to visit them as well. As a result, I believe our four children will carry fond memories of each of their grandparents.

While still in East Lansing, we purchased a small home-made trailer, and a friend built us a sturdy box fitted out as our camping kitchen. Albeit heavy, it contained enough cooking gear to meet our needs while camping in the various tents we used over the years. At the end of our year's sojourn in Michigan, Tom, had his diploma in hand, and we left for Guatemala for our second term. We drove, pulling our trailer, well-loaded with camping and other gear. Grandma and Grandpa Gyori agreed to travel with us in their car. A young woman friend also agreed to accompany us as an extra driver.

Traveling in tandem made this a memorable trip. When we reached Mexico City, the challenge to remain together outwitted poor Grandpa Julius, separating us in mid-city. Undaunted, Grandpa kept his cool, and we reconnected before finding our hotel for the night. Unfortunately, Julius's heart didn't like the altitude or pollution, or both, and he became very short of breath. We left early in the morning for Puebla and Vera Cruz. He was much improved after we descended into healthier altitudes.

CHAPTER 9

Second Term

> *How can young people keep themselves
>   on the straight and narrow?
> By keeping your words.*
>
> **PSALM 119:9**

We had agreed that we needed to live in Guatemala City in order to take advantage of school opportunities for the children. We had to find a place to live before deciding on a school. So, after Tom's parents returned home, we found a house in a development called Granai Townsend in zone 11 of the capital. Determined not to send any of our children away to a boarding school was a major reason to live in the city. We enrolled them in the Evelyn Rogers school, a bi-lingual primary school. Tom Jr. entered the 4th grade, Ken, 3rd, and Sonja, 1st. Later Jim enrolled in the kindergarten.

A couple of years later, the children complained about this school and pleaded with us to find something different. We consulted with our friends, Gloria and Ross Kinsler and found that they, too, were not happy with the school situation for their three children. We approached Barbara and Don

Weisbrod, a young couple who were living in Guatemala City and were both teachers by profession. Don was working with Tom in the development of Icthus, a new youth ministry for junior high boys. We floated the idea of their teaching our seven children in our own school. While in the States, I had done some research into "Open Schools" and visited at least one in Chicago, I was captivated by this alternative approach. This system did not rely on grades as a standard measurement of accomplishment and seemed an innovative and pragmatic approach to education. Children were encouraged to advance and explore typical subject materials at their individual pace, guided by our teachers. After much deliberation, Barbara and Don accepted our offer to pay them what we had been paying the Evelyn Rogers school, and they enthusiastically rose to the challenge.

The Integrated Day Center, or IDC, began in the Weisbrod's home with our seven children. Aware of the U.S. school requirements, we began to develop a new curriculum from scratch. This became an exciting adventure for me, particularly, since I had had no formal teacher training. But I had excellent role models! Our enrollment grew steadily, and we were privileged to capture the attention of a growing number of qualified teachers willing to embark on this educational experiment with us. Some were expatriates from the States, others were local Guatemalans. When we outgrew space in Babs' and Don's home, we rented a two-story building on a major avenue in the city. There we had the space and pleasant surroundings to expand and deepen our curriculum. There is no question that different children responded differently to the IDC. I had dreamt of a tri-lingual school but found it would be economically unfeasible. So Spanish and English ruled. Among our four children, it seems that Jim found this format of education the least fulfilling, but he suffered no lasting "scars." Babs later told me of how impressed she had been working with "Jimmy" as he was learning to read. She later wrote: "He was struggling with learning to read, and I was trying various approaches to encourage him. One day, while I was telling the kids a story at the end of the day, he stood up, found a piece of paper and pencil and wrote something on the paper. Then he walked over to where I was sitting, handed me the paper and said—or more accurately "demanded": (he was intense) "what does this say?" I took the paper and read his words back to him. He said: "That IS what it says." What struck me about the experience as a teacher is that he was building a hypothesis about what reading actually IS—mind to mind communication without the use of speech. Vowels and consonants are easy once you grasp that! Now, as the school counselor in a Chicago suburban high school, Jim is involved with the renovation of the entire school's curriculum. He commented that this reminds him of the IDC. Barbara has said what a significant experience it was for her, partly because we were not limited by bureaucratic boundaries.

As our students advanced to higher grade levels, I became the coordinator of the secondary section. Again, I found the challenge exciting and threw my whole self into this new adventure. Our enrollment was 50 students at the time of the closure of the IDC. Tom's unwavering support was key to my participation. I will always be enormously grateful for the ways Tom consistently fostered in me the courage to be myself, whether in exploring alternative health provision, secular and Christian education efforts, or later advocacy for human rights.

After Tom Jr. and Christy Porter had successfully completed their respective high school course work and taken the standard SAT and ACT exams in the American School, we made personalized diplomas for them and celebrated their graduation.

"It is this belief in a power larger than myself and other than myself which allows me to venture into the unknown and even the unknowable." These words by Maya Angelou articulate for me much of how I felt during our years in Guatemala. During that time her words became a part of my becoming myself, as I pursued alternatives in health care, educational strategies, and other "out of the box" endeavors. Is it part of the rebel within or my cavalier and blind tendency to follow current fads, or simply that I'm a subversive seed saver?

Earthquake

> *God is our refuge and our strength,*
>   *Who of old had helped us in our distress.*
> *Therefore we fear nothing_*
> *Even if the earth should open up in front of us*
>   *And mountains plunge into the depths of the sea,*
>   *Even if the earth's water rage and foam*
>   *And the mountains tumble with its heaving.*
> **PSALM 46:1–4**

A destructive earthquake measuring 7.5 degrees, on the Richter scale, wreaked havoc over a huge swath of Guatemala around 3 a.m. February 4, 1976. Normalcy, as we had known it, was shattered! Although the school building was not severely damaged, we had to close the IDC because too many student's families left the country and those of us who stayed became entirely enveloped in recovery efforts across the country.

The earthquake awakened Tom and Ken when books fell on them from the shelves above their heads, Jim felt water from the fish tank splattering on him and Sonja called all of us to stand in a doorway for protection. We were grateful that our home suffered no damage, but soon it was apparent neighbors were not so fortunate. At least one house bordering on a nearby ravine had fallen down the precipice. We joined others in the street and were terrified by the innumerable af-ter-shocks which shook us to the core.

Daylight revealed extensive damage in many neighbor-hoods of Guatemala City; it was even worse in towns and villages across the country. Guastatoya, El Progreso, was also hard hit. Tom and I went there in a VW bug as soon as possible and were diverted off the highway due to a collapsed bridge. We drove several miles through a shallow river, en route to our former hometown. Driving into a familiar town that has been demolished in one fell swoop during one night, left us feeling bereft! First on our agenda was to talk with our many friends in town, to assess their conditions. I do not remem-ber of many lives lost in Guastatoya despite the physical dam-age to homes and infrastructure. Significantly, one of the few buildings relatively undamaged was the Presbyterian Church. However, I don't recall it becoming a central location of relief efforts.

Tom became deeply involved in re-building efforts, both by the churches and by government agencies. I was impressed with the international aid that flowed in, with different countries committing to specific needs. One country offered corrugated steel roofing, another, road reconstruction, while another, assistance in building earthquake-proof homes. By and large, it seemed that these efforts were well coordinated and proved effective.

At the same time, we experienced frustration with individuals and groups offering inappropriate aid, needs for recognition, rather than the desire to respond to the felt needs of the affected populace. As always, a disaster of this magnitude brought forth the best and worst in people. Our non-stop investment of time and energy took its toll. We decided to bring the family to the States for the summer. We packed into our car, joined by Don Sibley, colleague and co-driver, and drove to Asheville, North Carolina, where my parents lived. The children and I remained there while Don and Tom returned to Guatemala.

In anticipation of our stay, Daddy bought an above ground swimming pool which we all thoroughly enjoyed during the hot days ahead. Another fond memory of that summer is the week the children and I camped at the Montreat Conference Center, a Presbyterian camp and conference facility, in nearby Montreat, North Carolina. We pitched our tent on a site bordering a fast-flowing spring, in which we cooled perishable food like milk and drinks. I had enrolled the children in the proffered children's programs while I participated in a music course led by the innovative church musicians, Avery and Marsh. How I enjoyed learning new hymns and singing

them and teaching them to my children! That was a memorably happy week for one and all, so much so that years later
we had an opportunity to drive through Montreat. Sonja, now
an adult, insisted that we revisit that campsite which she was
able to identify.

My sister Rosaline drove to Asheville, picked up the children and me and drove us to her home in Windsor, Ontario.
There we enjoyed being with her and her husband Fred, while
we awaited Tom's return to pick us up for our return to Guatemala. I don't know when I had looked forward to Tom's appearance with more joyful anticipation!

The drive back to Guatemala was another happy experience of about five days enjoying each other. I especially enjoyed reading to the children in the car. We pitched our tent
at night along the way. One night, we just stopped beside the
road because Tom became too weary to continue. Some tried
to sleep in the car, while others slept under our tarp outside.
The mosquitoes were so bad, no one could sleep, and finally
we could do none other than pile back into the car and continue on our way. This was only one of several times we drove
from Guatemala to the U.S. and back, a definite advantage to
being posted in a country relatively close by.

That fall we were again faced with the challenge of schooling for three of our children. Tom had finished high school.
He was preparing to go to Chicago to live with Grandma and
Grandpa Gyori, expecting to find work until he began his
studies at Warren Wilson College in North Carolina. Ken decided he wanted to have his senior year in high school at the
American School in Guatemala City, which is where he enrolled. He did very well there and graduated at the end of the

school year. He too, followed brother Tom's route and made his way to Chicago to work and live with Grandma and Grandpa Gyori. After a year, he also enrolled in Warren Wilson College. Jim returned to the Evelyn Rogers School where all four had attended previously.

Sonja and I agreed to create independent studies for her junior year in high school. This turned out to be an exciting challenge. We asked Barbara Weisbrod, co-founder of the IDC and a language arts teacher, if she would create a course in English literature for Sonja. She enthusiastically agreed. We then asked another expatriate who agreed to teach her physics. Sonja enrolled in the French Academy for language studies, in the national gymnastics center for physical education, and I tutored her in "home economics." She did very well in each of these courses and decided she wanted a "legitimate" high school diploma from a "real" school. So she conferred with the principal at the Evelyn Rogers School and defended the legitimacy of her junior year studies and was accepted. She graduated the following year as the salutatorian of her class. Upon her graduation, we were due for another furlough, so made our plans to return to Chicago.

CHAPTER 10

Learning to Drive

Despite my never driving a car, why was I willing to travel with at least Ken and Sonja, on their maiden voyages? I remember accompanying Ken as he drove the winding, back roads between Panajachel and Guatemala City. He did very well that time. But on a short drive from the beach near Champerico, Guatemala, up to Quetzaltenango, with the entire family aboard, he misjudged a sharp turn in a small town, scraping the passenger side of the car against a high mud brick embankment. Only superficial damage resulted.

Sonja's first venture of driving between Quetzaltenango and Guatemala City resulted in a more serious incident. She and I were alone in the car and as we climbed a long stretch, she hit a bicyclist also climbing the hill. Fortunately, he didn't seem injured, and I settled with him by giving him some money. I never felt happy about my response but didn't know what else to do under the circumstances.

Her second accident was also traumatic. She and Jim were returning home in the capital when she came to a four-way stop. Not knowing whose turn it was to go next, she started up simultaneously with the driver from her right. He hit the passenger door, where Jim sat. Again, no one was injured, but Sonja was thoroughly frightened. I remember Babs Weisbrod, a good friend and former teacher of Sonja's, counseled her to repeatedly tell her story of what happened, thus relieving her of her guilt and fear. Unfortunately, this happened just before we were preparing to leave Guatemala. Tom was not a happy camper, as he was trying to sell that car before we left.

Now at 88, I still don't drive! Fear and pregnancies aside, I now enjoy my resultant dependency on others for transportation. For the first time in my life, I live where there is no viable public transportation in the area. Also, I am more than aware of the way private cars enhance global warming significantly.

Enjoying innumerable, rich conversations, with family and friends is so rewarding. The issues of the independence offered by the private car, and dependency on others have been important lessons for me. Sonja, my most frequent chauffeur, continues to be both most generous and trusted to get me to church, for instance, and shopping from time to time. I try not to take advantage of her kindness. Asking for rides, has been a joy.

Both MegaBus and Greyhound are now my frequent distance transportation to Chicago and Ann Arbor, each trip having provided many humorous and challenging tales to tell.

Our Pets

It is important to include in this narrative the role animals played in our family during the previous 15 years. It seems as if we were never without at least one household pet. While living in Guastatoya, we enjoyed our beautiful German shepherd, Scamp, accompanying her through her pregnancy and delivery. We also had a succession of cats, some brighter than others. None were very "cuddly'" as I recall! We left Scamp with friends in Guatemala City during our first furlough where she was killed in an accident.

Our next residence was in the Granai Townsend neighborhood where we acquired Doli. He was a friendly, British border collie. He soon endeared himself to us all and became a beloved member of our family. We left Doli with friends during our second furlough and happily greeted him again upon our return. While living in Zone 2, we acquired several pets, including an iguana and a rabbit. Sonja bought a baby yellow crested parrot in the market, whom we named Max. She and Max were inseparable, and he quickly built an amazing bi-lingual vocabulary. Max much preferred female humans to males. His best friend, however, was Hoppy, the rabbit, who we kept in a caged area in the back yard. Max had a perch above the cage, and frequently flew down to join Hoppy. Much family lore developed around these assorted animals as time passed, especially around Max's antics.

What to do with Max and Doli became a major issue when we prepared to return to the States. The children were adamant about including them in our passage out of Guatemala, so Tom went all the way up to the minister of agriculture to get permission to take Max to the U.S. The letter he delivered had all but Sonja's tears imprinted. After yet another rejection, Tom mentioned our plight to our friendly travel agent who assured him, "No problem, I know so-and-so at the airport who will authorize Max's exit." With Max taken care of, Tom proceeded to build a box/cage for Doli for his plane ride. It was a lovely box complete with window, etc.

As we were waiting for our delayed flight at the airport, Tom looked out of the window at our plane which had the baggage hold open, and saw Doli barking away, outside his cage. Upon notifying an employee, Tom went into the plane and boarded up the cage more securely with an unhappy Doli inside. Because of the delay of the flight, we missed our connecting flight in Miami to Chicago. The decision was made for Tom to stay behind with the animals while I boarded another flight home, with the children. Poor Doli never outlived the trauma of being caged for so long! Max was kept in quarantine awaiting the morning flight to Chicago. In the end they all arrived safe and sound.

CHAPTER 11

Transition Time for All

> I will thank you with an upright heart,
>   when I truly learn to be as just
>   as you want me to be.
> I will obey your statutes;
>   do not utterly forsake me.
>
> PSALM 119:7,8

Arriving back in the United States was daunting and unsettling, to say the least. I remember feeling like Sarah, as in Abraham and Sarah who upon being "called" to leave Ur of the Caldeas, ventured into an unknown country, an unknown future, and were completely at God's mercy! That's how foreign or strange returning to the U.S. felt to me, rather than coming home. What did our future hold?

Reflecting back on the previous 22 years of my life was not an exercise of introspection I engaged in at this time. However, thinking back on the year of 1957, I recognize how dramatically my life had changed since marrying Tom. An explosion of new learnings, experiences, and commitments defined those years. How young and naive Tom and I were when we pledged our troths to one another on September 7, 1957!

Our mutual love and respect carried us through seminary, the birth of children, life-forming decisions, and the surprises of accepting a God-inspired call to Guatemala. Once there, becoming adept in using a new language, becoming acquainted with missionary co-workers, discerning directions of new professional engagements, engaging with our new Guatemalan friends and colleagues and learning how to enable the development of our growing family became all-encompassing chores—all filled with gratifying rewards as well as their particular challenges. In totality this was exciting, liberating, and humbling all at once. I have recently become aware of how our Guatemalan colleagues, Julia Esquivel, Gilo Mendez, Samuel Mejia, Edgardo and Yolanda Garcia, Julio Paz, Rosario y David de Leon, and Jose Luis Saguil among others, had become our professors in the University of Life.

No wonder I felt completely at a loss upon returning to the United States! How could life here begin to measure up to the plethora of opportunities which seemed to abound for me in Guatemala? Our maturing children would be making few and different demands on me. How could I practice, or grow in my new theological awakening spawned by Liberation Theology? Who would/could understand? How could or should I share the cataclysmic changes that had occurred in me, and with whom? Politically, my acquired awareness in experiencing the devastating influences my government held in Central America, were still developing and how to express these concerns to family and friends in Chicago? What difference could I make?

Another area was my newly developed creativity, challenging the status quo in theological and secular education, in western styled medical preparation, and a nascent, yet important dawning awareness of our place, living in and with God's good creation. What opportunities might present themselves, what was my calling in this unexplored environment?

Chicago/Skokie

> I'll teach you and show you the way you should walk;
> I will counsel you, and keep watch over you.
> Be wise!
>
> **PSALM 32:8**

We were warmly welcomed by Tom's mom where more adventures awaited us as we all crammed into Grandma Gyori's small two-bedroom apartment, including Doli and Max. During the summer that we lived at 3913 N. St. Louis, we shared memorable moments together. Beth Kinsler joined us. She is the daughter of our friends Ross and Gloria Kinsler and Sonja's close friend from Guatemala. Beth had come from Geneva, Switzerland, where her family was living at the time. She and Sonja slept in the basement for the summer and they both found jobs in the city. We still wonder how we managed, rather how Grandma withstood this mass invasion into her space! We had to keep Max quarantined for 90 days until the designated official came to inspect the bird and give clearance.

Beth returned home, Tom Jr. returned to Warren Wilson with Ken who had also enrolled there. We found an apartment in Skokie, just north of Chicago. There we enrolled Jim, as an eighth grader in the local school, which was not a happy transition for him. He made us promise not to mention Guatemala, and never speak Spanish around his school friends.

He wanted to blend in as quickly and easily as possible. This was particularly difficult because Skokie was a close-knit, predominantly Jewish community, in which many of his classmates had been together for much of their grade school years. It was not easy breaking into that scene, especially having just left Guatemala, his home and natal country. He proved his resilience and made the best of a difficult situation.

Doli had a more difficult time. He literally seemed to go berserk whenever we left him alone, tearing apart curtains, furniture and even a door! Max became a challenge, especially to Tom Jr. Max always favored women to men, so after "attacking" Tom once too many times, Tom literally threw the bird down the stairs! No damage done to the bird.

Grandma Gyori's mettle was thoroughly challenged by our pets. We had to leave them with her from time to time as we went shopping or other errands. One time, Doli escaped under the back fence. Upon returning to Grandma's, we all searched the neighborhood in vain. Discouraged, we returned to Skokie without him. A phone call interrupted our dinner. The caller said they had found Doli wandering in the street, miles from home, and following information from his collar, they found us. Tom and Sonja followed their instructions to their home in a nearby suburb. During an extended conversation, these friendly folk said they were related to the Durkovicks, Lutheran missionaries in Guatemala. Sonja had baby-sat the Durkovic children, and we were good friends, living near them in Guatemala City. This interchange only enhanced our joy at recovering Doli. Unfortunately, it became evident that Doli was just too unhappy with the confinement of living in a big city, so we had to give him away.

1980: An Exciting Year!

The innumerable questions which plagued me last year about what in the world would I do back in the States, were smothered in the incredible events that transpired in the Gyori family in 1980! Upon releasing 25 journals from their hibernation in boxes spanning almost 40 years, I opened the first, and largest one which began with the words, "Today I begin the journey of journaling." The date, January 25, 1980. I was little prepared for the journey that unfolded before me!

In early April, Sonja accepted Beth Kinsler's invitation to visit her in Geneva and accompany her and Rachel Sibley in exploring Italy, Greece, and other points south of Geneva. In the meantime, before leaving Chicago, the Kinslers included me in the invitation to visit them. With Grandma Gyori's generous help, I joined Sonja in Geneva upon their return from their southern adventures.

Words seem so inadequate to begin to relate the bonding, joys, and challenges Sonja and I shared during the ensuing two weeks Eurailing across Europe together. We caught an early train leaving Geneva for Marburg, Germany. There we were warmly greeted by Linda and Rainer, a couple we had known in Guatemala. They drove us to their home and then took us to West Berlin, where we met Rainer's good friend, Harold who lived there.

The three of them took us all over both East and West Berlin, a brand new, learning experience for both Sonja and I. The tragic history of a divided Germany came to life, as we walked along the dividing wall between east and west. Albeit all too brief, we did get a short glimpse of life under Communism's planned and controlled economy. Time spent in an

East German Museum showed us the rationale given by the communists for building the wall. Having Harold share his insights into all of this, was marvelous. What a grand time we enjoyed with these three vibrant, intelligent students!

We took trains north to Amsterdam. There we faced the challenge of whether to stay in the hostel we had chosen, which turned out to be in the heart of Amsterdam's renowned "red light district"! We found the place clean, and more than adequate for our needs. After eating our usual fare of bread, cheese and yogurt, we packed up, took our bags to the railroad station where we stored them in a storage facility, and began an incredibly beautiful experience! We walked through breathtakingly stunning gardens, artistically planted with tulips, daisies, hyacinths, blue bells, jonquils and more tulips. From there we looked over acres and acres of tulips and hyacinths spread over vast spaces of the countryside. We were gifted with more vistas of floral fields from the train window as we finally left and made our way to Paris.

Our time in Paris turned out to be a huge disappointment due to a strike of museum employees. We walked through manicured gardens surrounding the Louvre, Versailles, Eifel Tower, and of course down the Champs Elise. We enjoyed a break from our bread and cheese and had a good dinner on our American Express card, after having spent most of our francs.

On May 10, we arrived in San Sebastian, Spain, finding a small pension near the beach. The first morning there we splurged with a breakfast of eggs, fruit, croissants and coffee. Many happy hours were spent sunning on the beach, walking through fascinating small streets, and thoroughly relaxing and enjoying ourselves. Plans to travel west to Santander were thwarted but we explored some nearby towns for a couple of days. The most challenging travel confronted us as we tried to make our way back to Geneva in time for Sonja to fly out on May 15. Missing some trains, rerouting through Paris after a train strike ended there, we finally arrived in Geneva at 12:30 a.m. and were met by Ross Kinsler. then Sonja caught her plane home that morning.

I had the privilege of staying on for another week with the Kinslers. Before Ross had to leave for Australia, he took me to the World Council of Churches' office building, showed me around and introduced me to several interesting people. I also met a gentleman working in the World Health Organization building where again I had some good conversations, always pursuing future work opportunities for us. Ben Gutierrez had said something about medical work in Colombia, so I asked around for more information on this, to no satisfactory end, however. It was all very interesting and new for me. Gloria took me for a short stay in a Swiss chalet, where we enjoyed each other's company, to say nothing of the extravagant scenery in the Alps, a most refreshing and renewing time together. I bid them all a sad farewell on the 23rd and flew home.

About six weeks after returning home, Tom and I flew to Guatemala to finalize our affairs there. It seemed clear to us that continuing to work there was not to be, despite the invitation of the North Presbytery. That document apparently was never brought forward during the Synod meeting in which a future assignment for us was to have been acted upon. We packed the things we had left for shipping to the U.S. In like fashion as upon our initial arrival in Guatemala 15 years prior, Tom and I made a grand tour of the country visiting colleagues, now including beloved Guatemalan friends as well as compatriots. What rich conversations we had in each encounter reliving common memories, saying sad farewells and enjoying again this magnificent country with its awe-inspiring landscapes, varied climates, astounding history, and above all its incomparably colorful and complicated diversity of people. It's impossible not to fall in love with Guatemala! We asked many questions of different friends about the growing, impending conflict which was about to engulf the entire country in a decade of bloody, civil strife. Responses ranged from strong criticisms of U.S. policies to hopeful expectations of the Second Coming!

Upon saying good-bye to our home for fifteen years, we flew to Colombia where we were warmly welcomed in Cartagena by our good friends, the Cuthberts. Unfortunately, no one in the church knew anything about our arrival even though Ben Gutierrez met us there to explore work opportunities. Poor timing, planning and communication left us unwilling to pursue this option further.

This transition year for Tom and I living in Skokie was filled with speaking in related churches, and discerning where God was calling us. In the meantime, we found ourselves trying to relate major mission issues like hunger, human rights, justice and peace as we had observed them in Guatemala, to the lives of our fellow Presbyterians in the states. Not an easy task!

I was invited to serve on the governing board of the Program Agency of the Presbyterian Church, which was a valuable learning experience for me, involving travel to meetings in New York and elsewhere. However, it seemed clear to me that serving the church at these levels was not my calling, so upon finishing designated terms, I looked for other avenues of service.

CHAPTER 12

Following God's Call

> *How I rejoiced when they said to me,*
> *"Let us go to the house of our God."*
>
> **PSALM 122:1**

The first opportunity came when Tom was called to serve as the interim pastor of the Lake View Presbyterian Church in Chicago. Tom had been hired by the Presbytery of Chicago to serve as a liaison between the presbytery and the Hispanic congregations within its bounds. That included serving as an interim pastor when there was a vacancy. In 1980 all Hispanic pulpits were filled, hence the invitation to work at Lake View. This was a dying congregation on the near north side of the city. The faithful few, however, were a determined, rather progressive bunch, and we felt at home there. I joined the church and eventually was ordained as a ruling elder. Here I found a spiritual home, which I had not had in years.

As I read my journals through 1982, I noticed significant shifts in my personal theology, understanding of my call as a Christian, my family relationships, and growing concerns and activities around advocacy in Central America, my theological growth was informed and enlivened, to say nothing of being challenged by the Covenant Community (C.C.) in Evanston, led by Rev. Bud Ogle. Having met Bud and some others in C.C. during a visit from them in Guatemala previously, Bud invited us to join this group of progressive Christians living and working around Northwestern University in Evanston, Illinois. We were introduced to intentional community living, feminist theology, non-violence as a way of living, and broader international advocacy as in Palestine and South Africa, to name some new areas of concern. Articulating my Christology, biblical understanding of Christian faith, and how that all needs to be lived out pragmatically, became imperative activities for me. I found the writing of my personal theological beliefs at this time remains consistent with my current affirmations. Becoming an active participant in Chicago protest rallies with C.C. folk, was a new and exciting experience for me. My transition to living in the states was a fruitful one. Advocacy for human rights in Central American was now perceived to be my calling, a new way to use my gifts.

As to family relationships, I found in my journals all too frequent criticisms of Tom. I wanted him to become more politically active, more articulate in his preaching, and basically more conforming to my ideals and wishes. This was unfair on my part. I expressed concerns about my ability to communicate with sons Tom and Jim, especially, trying to be as affirming of each in particular scholastic and interpersonal challenges. Jim lived with us during his high school years and that was a wonderful learning experience for all three of us.

A significant opportunity arose when I was invited to join a Presbyterian General Assembly Task Force on Central

America, We were to visit the region and prepare a policy statement to be presented at the upcoming General Assembly meeting. It would articulate our denomination's stand on our country's involvement in events happening in Central America, The year was 1982, and the Task Force met in New York in July and in Washington in September, in preparation for our visits to Mexico, Guatemala, El Salvador, Nicaragua, and Costa Rica in November. I seriously questioned the wisdom of going to Guatemala which was embroiled in a brutal conflict between the government of General Rios Mont and the Indigenous people. Hundreds of Guatemalans fled into neighboring Chiapas, Mexico, where they lived under the protection of the United Nations.

Reading some of the letters I wrote to our denominational leaders, I am impressed with my courage to pose critical questions to them. The Presbyterian Church of Guatemala was preparing to celebrate its centennial, with officials from the PCUSA scheduled to be present. Rev. Jim Costen was the moderator of our General Assembly and the designated representative of our US denomination at the official centennial celebrations. He and his wife did go, and I accompanied them in Mexico City before their entry into Guatemala.

After meeting with members of the State Department, the Heritage Foundation, Congress people, university representatives, former ambassador Robert White and leaders of solidarity groups, The General Assembly Task Force felt prepared to fulfill this adventurous mandate. I recall the prayerful, agonizing discussion we had in Mexico City, trying to decide if the task force should send a representative to Guatemala and if so, who should go. Finally, I agreed to serve in that role and won't soon forget the experience! We were met at the airport and whisked away to the Pan American Hotel in the heart of Guatemala City. There we met clandestinely in a darkened hotel room with music playing to drown out our whispered conversation with friend Dennis Smith, and Rev. Jose Carrera, a recognized statesman of the Guatemalan Presbyterian Church. Rev. Carerra, or Don Chepe, as he was lovingly named, and Dennis shared with us sobering details of the raging conflict and how it was affecting the church. I was profoundly moved because of our first-hand experiences in the country with these two men and in that place. The biggest conundrum for me was the apparent wide-spread support among religious leaders, both protestant and catholic, for President Efrain Rios Mont, a self-declared Christian. He has subsequently been held accountable for the destruction of over forty Mayan communities, all in the name of anti-communism.

We interviewed one of President Mont's top officials. We asked about the extrajudicial killings of so many rural people. His response stunned us. "They deserve to die for having become communists, siding with the guerillas," he explained.

The centennial celebrations of the Guatemalan Presbyterian Church were enjoyed without any interference.

We spent several days visiting other countries in Central America and took time in Costa Rica to begin to formulate our report. We decided to use the biblical story of the road to Emma-us as the framework for the final position paper. We were more than satisfied with the final product, which indeed became the guiding document forming our denomination's response to U.S. involvement in the region.

Rev. John Fife, a fellow member of our group, asked me to extend my stay in order to accompany him as his translator. We meet with Guatemalan refugees as they were fleeing into Mexico. We sat in a field on the border of Guatemala and Mexico, near Tapachula, and listened to the heart-rending stories shared by several refugees. They told about the terror they felt as government bombs exploded in the center of their villages, killing family members and leaving no other option but to flee across the border.

John was the pastor of Southside Presbyterian Church in Tucson, Arizona, which was the first church to declare itself a sanctuary congregation to house refugees fleeing Central America, How much did our time sitting on that border influence the decision to start this law-defying movement? Later when Tom and I visited this church, John spotted us in the congregation and publicly welcomed us with, "Grace and I slept together across Central America!"

Witness for Peace

Turn away from bad and practice good;
Seek peace and pursue it.

PSALM 34:14

Due to my experience in Central America, I responded positively to an invitation to join a large delegation of 200 people, from the United States, to visit Nicaragua, in 1983. The full-fledged conflict between the Sandinista government in Nicaragua and the U. S. backed Contras was becoming headline news. The organizers of this large delegation wondered if the presence of such a large group of U.S. religious persons might serve as a protective shield for Nicaraguans caught in this fighting. Gail Phares, a seasoned activist from Raleigh, NC, was the primary organizer of this national call. Sojourners Community in Washington D.C. was an active co-sponsor of this initiative.

I was enthusiastic about this call and was initiated into still another career, that of a political activist. The mere size of this delegation made it memorable, as did the thorough planning and organizing of logistics. We gathered in Washington, D.C., for our orientation, where I met some remarkable new friends. Also, son Tom and his wife Lisa drove from Raleigh for the commissioning service held in the National Cathedral. The service introduced powerful new hymns which became indelibly written into my memory. As we sang "Here I am Lord, It is I Lord…" I felt I was indeed responding to a call from God.

Attending to over 200 "gringos" in Nicaragua, presented a formidable challenge to local folks there! Some examples stand out. One noon time meal of roasted chicken was being prepared for us before we were to board buses to take us to Jalapa, on the border with Honduras. Our hosts ran out of food and we had to wait. Bread was in short supply due to lack of available flour. While we were waiting, I was sitting on a bus and saw a familiar figure walk past, toting a backpack. I recognized him to be the well-known theologian, Henri Nouwen! He was traveling alone in Nicaragua and asked to join us to go up North. Of course, he was welcomed! Later upon arriving in Jalapa at supper time, we were eating in a school building where we were housed. We had been divided into groups corresponding to different areas of our origins in the U.S. I was the leader of the Central Mid-West region. As we were finishing our meal, and were deeply engaged in conversation, Nouwen quietly came in and, slowly walked around the circle relieving us of our empty plates and taking them to the kitchen. This extended our time together by an important few minutes.

The organizers of this delegation were deeply concerned about the United States' support of the Contras, a right-wing rebel group whose mission was to defeat the military of the duly elected Sandinsta government of Nicaragua. The U.S. government considered the Sandinistas a communist threat to the region. After untold numbers of casualties and major disruption in Nicaragua, the Contras were defeated in 1990,

Jalapa and the border area was where the Contras were actively engaging with Sandinista forces. An incident I remember well, was our meeting with the U.S. ambassador to Nicaragua. We presented him with well-articulated questions about U.S. policies and support of the contras, and the resulting devastation to so many Nicaraguan lives. He was hard pressed to give us satisfactory responses.

Witness for Peace, WFP, was born from this delegation. Before leaving Nicaragua, we began national organizing, and defining goals and objectives. A board of directors resulted, regional coordinators volunteered, and staff, housed with Sojourners in Washington were soon hired. I became the coordinator for the Central Midwest Region which included Iowa, Wisconsin, Illinois, Michigan, Indiana and Ohio. I also served on the national board of directors. WFP soon agreed that trying to provide a "protective shield" from the Contras was too arrogant a stand, rather we focused on organizing delegations from the different regions of the U.S. to travel to Nicaragua on a regular basis, to accompany people and to document the results of U.S. policies in the country. Upon returning to our own country, we committed to spreading the word of how our national policies were having such devastating effects on Nicaraguans. Communicating our findings and experiences to our elected officials was also a major task. We succeeded in finally changing our nation's foreign policy and averted a U.S. invasion of Nicaragua. Together we were learning what da Vinci meant when he warned us, "Nothing strengthens authority so much as silence." We were determined to break the silence of our government's military activities in small countries like Nicaragua.

For the next 10 years, these activities engaged me full time. I established an office in our basement, from which I organized delegations from our region and organized our volunteer state leaders. I also communicated with WFP staff and delegates as well as led innumerable delegations myself, to Nicaragua and Central America.

For me, WFP represented an exposure to and appreciation of the rich tapestry of different faiths, all united in articulating and living a just and faithful life. Among our leadership were Jews, Christians, Buddhists, agnostics and more, who provided well-grounded inspiration for pursuing often risky adventures. This variety of faith expressions enriched and emboldened my Christian commitment to Jesus' life and example of peacemaking.

Besides the frequent delegations of volunteers who traveled to Nicaragua for two weeks, we had a strong contingent of "long term" volunteers who lived and worked throughout Nicaragua who serviced the short-term delegations, but more importantly became intimately involved in local communities at risk throughout the country. I offered a listening ear as they processed these traumatic events after returning home. Several books, songs, and other publications have resulted from our experiences.

How effective was all this effort by WFP in the long run? Did our activities shorten the Contra war? How many policy makers were influenced by Witness for Peace? I am not aware of any statistical measures which can answer these questions. We were convinced that we were at least faithful in attempts to call our nation to accountability for its policies in Central America. We are convinced that WFP indeed averted a prolonged U.S. war in Nicaragua.

CHAPTER 13

Our Children are Growing Up

> *Children are the heritage God gives us;*
> *Our descendants are our rewards.*
>
> **PSALM 127:3**

On May 14, 1983, Tom Jr. graduated from North Carolina State University, having majored in computer science. He holds the honor of being the first of our children to marry. On a cloudy, rainy Oct. 22, 1983, Tom married Lisa Whitney in Evanston, Illinois. The inclement weather did little to dampen their joy in beginning a new life together! Tom Sr. was invited to participate in the wedding in Westminster Presbyterian Church in Evanston. After their honeymoon, Lisa and Tom moved to Raleigh, North Carolina, where they have lived ever since. Lisa became employed in the public school system as a specialist with visually impaired students. Tom gained employment with a visionary "start up" group SAS, where he continues to expand his computer skills to this day.

Ken graduated with honors in May 1983, from Macalester College in St. Paul, Minnesota. He then accepted an internship with National Geographic in Washington, DC, in their cartography department. In the fall semester of his junior year at Macalester, he spent September-December 1981, in Colombia. Following his semester abroad, he decided to do additional travel across South America over the next two months, ending up in Brazil. Being an adventurous soul, he chose to cross the continent by train from Bolivia into Brazil. Unfortunately, he did not get a visa to enter Brazil, so had to return on the same train to Bolivia. On the return trip to Brazil he wrote, "I've reached the end of my Kenhood!" Clearly, he was near his limit of determination. Such was his disappointment to have to make that extra travel on the "chicken train."

Upon arriving in Sao Paulo, he contacted some Presbyterian missionaries, who helped him find his way around that sprawling metropolis. One of his Colombian classmates had urged Ken to look up her cousin who lived in Sao Paolo. Ken soon knocked on Beatriz Fusco's door and met the love of his life. Bea's family welcomed him warmly and added to the joy of his first visit to Brazil. He had applied for a Fulbright scholarship to work in Colombia but was directed by Fulbright to Brasilia, Brazil, instead! Leaving National Geographic, he headed south to study the lives of Brazilians who had been hired to build that new capital city from scratch. He made short work of reuniting with Bea, and their relationship matured into a commitment to live their lives as one.

While Ken was living and working in Brasilia, Tom and I flew to Brazil to visit him and to meet his fiance. Bea and her parents welcomed us into their lovely home in Sao Paulo. We were treated royally; they introduced us to some of their favorite places in and around Sao Paulo. Bea amazed us with her expertise, driving us around that enormous city of so many million residents, at times even resorting to driving on sidewalks to get where she wanted to go! Once she stopped in the middle of the street without batting an eye, jumped out of the car, and bought some sugar cane juice from a vendor who was prepared to quickly attend a customer.

Ken took us aside one evening and urgently asked Tom to please ask Jose, Bea's dad, for his permission to allow Bea to accompany us to Brasilia and spend the night with us so she could help show us around the capital. He didn't know Ken had already purchased bus tickets for all four of us. Jose was unwilling to give his consent that evening, saying he had to confer with Laura, his wife, and would let us know in the morning. Fortunately, they agreed and we enjoyed a couple of days in the gleaming new city in the center of the country.

Upon returning to Chicago, Ken was hired to work in the Chicago Presbytery office for the summer. He carefully planned their wedding to be held at Ravenswood Presbyterian Church, in Chicago, where Tom was serving as pastor. Bea and Laura arrived a week before the big day. The happy couple were married in a lovely ceremony. Thus began a brand-new life for Bea, in a strange country where she was surrounded by only English speakers, living in our home with her new husband until they moved into an empty seminary housing apartment in Hyde Park. It was an unhappy summer for her, what with many adjustments before her, with neither family nor friends to share lonely hours and days, while Ken was away at work. Both Tom and I were busy with our respective commitments and lived across town so were unable to spend enough time with her. Ken had enrolled in a master's program at the University of Texas in Dallas-Fort Worth. They moved into an apartment in Plano, near the university. We bade them farewell as they s drove our little VW "bug," pulling a trailer loaded with all their earthly belongings!

Sonja's story would be incomplete without talking more about her pet parrot, Max. She had received permission from Whitworth College in Spokane, Washington, where she had enrolled, to bring Max with her. Amtrak would not allow the bird on the train, so he had to be left behind, in Chicago. That meant we had to care for him. He and I got along fairly well. It wasn't long before he started mimicking my voice on the many telephone conversations I had with Witness for Peace friends, among others. In talking with a friend on the east coast, I was asked if we had an infant in the house. "No," was my response, "you are hearing Max, our parrot." He had a wide vocabulary, "Sonja, Sonja" was a favorite. Some Spanish phrases learned in Guatemala stuck with her. "Hello", "How are you?" was a frequent question. Her words and antics have become part of our family lore.

We were grateful that Sonja was able to receive substantial scholarship assistance. Sonja was unhappy at Whitworth, she was too far from home, and she had decided to pursue a nursing career. That major was not offered at Whitworth, and she transferred to Goshen College, a Mennonite school in Goshen, Indiana. There she was able to complete a nursing degree. One day she heard a young man saying something in her beloved Spanish, riding down the street on his bicycle. Turns out he was Ray Helmuth, son of missionaries to Puerto Rico. She pursued him, and he her, until they fell in love and after graduation were happily married in Goshen, in a simple wedding. She had made her wedding dress and asked friends and family to bake cakes and bring other dishes for a wedding picnic. Prior to the wedding, Ken had scoured the rural roads for flowers to decorate with, and a beautiful celebration ensued.

In the meantime, Jim was enrolled in Luther North High School in Chicago, where he enjoyed sports, especially wrestling, and made some lasting friends. He lived at home and relished the company of his pet snake, a python. Jim regularly obtained a mouse from a nearby pet shop and kept the snake well-fed and cared for in a large aquarium. One day it escaped, and I had to call Jim home from school to help me find him. Who wants to have a loose python slithering around your home? The snake was found coiled happily in the springs of my favorite recliner in the living room!

Following high school, Jim attended several universities and colleges before settling on the pursuit of a degree in physical education. He graduated from Northeastern University in Chicago. Later he returned to receive his master's degree in counseling. After finishing college, Jim, who seemed to want to stay in Chicago, surprised us and accepted a teaching position in St. Thomas in the U.S. Virgin Islands. Within days of arriving on the island, a hurricane swept through, frightening him and his roommate; they were not injured, and their apartment was unscathed.

Jim's days were happy ones, filled with teaching physical education and swimming, boating and generally enjoying the lovely beaches. Tom and I took advantage of his living in such an idyllic place by visiting for a few days. He proved to be an attentive host, reserving a romantic tent/cabin for us on St. John's Island for a night. We rented a small motorboat and cruised through the pristine waters, exploring brilliant white sand beaches and of course swimming.

After a year on St. Thomas, he accepted a teaching position in a private school in Quito, Ecuador. While there he made the acquaintance of Viviana Torres, who was teaching in the same school. Soon they fell in love and were married in an extravagant wedding in Quito. His siblings and spouses joined them for that lovely event. His young nephew Paul served as a ring bearer. Tom was honored to officiate in the outdoor wedding on a beautiful afternoon.

Jim and Vivi lived in Quito for a year before moving back to Chicago to establish their home. They brought their German Shepherd, Sparky, with them. Several years after they bought their first home near Chicago, their children, Niko and Isabella, were born and grew into active children. One day Niko ran inside exclaiming, "Mom, Isabella is all covered with dirt!" Investigating, Vivi discovered that toddler Isabella had been playing with some of Sparky's poop and managed to spread it generously over her body! That was the last straw for Vivi! She wanted no more to do with Sparky, and they threatened to turn her in to the local dog pound. When we learned of this, Tom and I convinced them to give Sparky to us. We were living at Loma Linda, our home in Beverly Shores, Indiana. Sparky became our beloved pet until she became old, and we had to have her put down. Tom Jr. was visiting us that day and helped Tom carry Sparky down the steps to the car, where she rested in the back seat with her head in my lap, as we drove to our vet in town. A sad day indeed!

CHAPTER 14

Living Full Lives in Chicago

Praise Our God, all you nations, extol
  God, all you mighty ones.
For God's love toward us is great.
God's faithfulness, eternal. Alleluia!

PSALM 117: 1,2

Tom and I were hardly sitting idly by, watching our four young adults mature and begin independent living with their respective spouses. Life took on ever greater challenges for each of us.

Upon reading my journal for the year 1982, I noted the variety and extent of my activities as an advocate for human rights in Central America, The ongoing challenge of interpreting this commitment in a meaningful way to local congregations compelled me to hone my speaking skills, and keep relevant and updated on the news of the escalating violence in the region. One memorable event was the Presbyterian Womens' triennial gathering at Purdue University. Two friends from Guatemala had been invited to participate, one being Julia Esquivel, a poet, and my theological mentor. She addressed the 5,000 women present, telling of the tragic devastation being wrought on Guatemala by the Rios Mont regime. Her heart-rending stories of the burning of innumerable villages and homes, the disruptions of family life and the terror as women, children and men fled for their lives into inhospitable jungles en route to the Mexican border. After Julia's presentation, the representative of the Presbyterian Women of Guatemala complained about the negative picture Julia had painted and commented on Jesus' words "the poor you will have with you always". She was one who supported Rios Mont because of his Christian identity and failed to challenge his racial policies of eliminating the population whom he depicted as communist sympathizers.

A much-needed reprieve occurred in September of 1982 when Tom and I celebrated our 25th wedding anniversary. We packed our camping gear and our bikes and drove east to Bar Harbor, Maine. There we set up camp on a piece of undeveloped property owned by two members of the Covenant Community. The ground was covered with low blueberry bushes, which provided us with a delicious accompaniment to our meals. I thoroughly enjoyed camping: the challenges of cooking special meals, wood gathering and fire building, organizing the site, relaxing in a hammock, and above all, being outdoors!

One day after a leisurely blueberry pancake breakfast, we chose a bike route on Mt. Desert Island. As we biked along beautiful trails, discovering exciting marvels of God's creation, we kept extending our route. The waterfalls, Jordon Pond, pine forests, and stands of birch, filled our hearts with joy. For supper that evening, we brought back to the campsite a cooked lobster which we enjoyed around a lovely fire. The grand finale to a wonderful day! Our children joined us there, except for Jim, and shared this milestone in our lives.

My journal entries in 1983 contained intriguing information about my ongoing discernment process and attempts to be sensitive to and guided by regular scriptural explorations into what might be God's ongoing direction. It was a year of frenetic activity on my part, as I responded to invitations to speak and teach about developments in Central America, I tried to elicit active responses from primarily Presbyterian churches but also from ecumenical groups. I agonized over the U.S. involvement in the distinct events in each country. Guatemala's challenge was the ongoing support of Christians for self-acclaimed Christian, President Efrain Rios Mont, as he engaged in systematic destruction of Indigenous people there. Christians in and out of Guatemala seemed unable to criticize him because he was such a convincing communicator of his Christian faith. The U.S. support of the Contras in Nicaragua was causing havoc there; Witness for Peace was founded to become a critical source of information to the people of our country about President Reagan's considerable funding of and logistical support for their attacks on civilian populations in Nicaragua. El Salvador continued in its deadly civil war during that year, also. My challenge was to interpret all of this to my compatriots in the U.S. I had varying degrees of "success."

In Chicago, I helped organize a Presbytery Task Force on Central America, We organized a rapid response network among ecumenical partners to respond to atrocities in El Salvador. We named it Christian Urgent Action Network, CUANES. The Presbytery of Chicago hired Gary Cozette to be our "point person" in El Salvador. He reported concerning incidents he was able to verify and shared these with our growing telephone network across the country. My involvement with Witness for Peace intensified as I organized and led delegations, primarily to Nicaragua.

Early in 1983, I was ordained a ruling elder in the Lake View Presbyterian Church. I welcomed that opportunity to be an active member of a local congregation after so many years of serving the wider denomination. This presented its own challenges. Even though Lake View was a progressive, albeit very small, congregation, I never felt comfortable about imposing a controversial issue on the members, notwithstanding the passion I felt about the conflicts in Central America and about our country's intimate involvement there.

With these experiences behind me, it was a natural fit to become involved with the nascent Sanctuary Movement organized in Tucson, and now extending to Chicago and across the nation. I became active in the Chicago Metropolitan Sanctuary Alliance and soon encouraged Lake View Presbyterian Church (LVPC) to agree to join the Alliance. LVPC didn't have living space to house immigrants seeking safety, so we teamed up with the near-by Wellington Avenue United Church of Christ and sponsored two Guatemalan refugees. We developed sophisticated security and legal measures to guarantee the safety of these two individuals. Their living space in the Wellington Church could only be accessed by a drop-down staircase. For a period of time, we stationed people in the building 24/7 in order to guard that area. We took turns accompanying our Guatemalan friends on speaking tours to other churches and to solidarity events. We were both translators and guards.

We provided for their physical needs, as well as protection services, all staffed by volunteers. Several other churches became active in the Sanctuary Alliance with us. Some chose to ensure accurate press coverage.

In November, I was offered the opportunity to return to Nicaragua with a Witness for Peace delegation. This time our group would be returning to the Honduran border where active fighting was happening. I agonized over my response, writing, "This is not a decision to be taken lightly. I need to look at my fears. I've never been in a life-threatening situation before. I think I can trust God's call and God's will with this. I do want to be an instrument of God's peace. That's my overriding motivation. I want to incarnate for other Christians, resistance to the evils perpetrated by our government. Is that being arrogant? Another motivation is to raise the ante for the Presbytery of Chicago. Will it get off its duff and seriously wrestle with the issues of war and peace? If my going could ignite a spark in that process, I would be eternally grateful." I did go, and it was indeed a profoundly moving and at times a harrowing experience.

Upon my return, I was scheduled to speak to a winter assembly of the Presbytery of Chicago. Tom took me directly from the airport to a stunning Gothic church in a northern suburb. As we entered the church, the magnificent pipe organ was playing Christmas music. The contrast with the scenes I had just left behind in Nicaragua came as an overwhelming shock. On the agenda for the day was a resolution in which Chicago Presbytery articulated a response to U.S. policies in Central America, with particular focus on our government's support of the Contras. Like an intimidated cat, I arose from sitting on the floor in a corner of a corridor. I ascended to the pulpit to address this august body. Principally, I shared with those present, my experience while riding a bus between Jalapa and Esteli in northern Nicaragua, near the Honduran border. We had been delayed in leaving Jalapa because there was open fighting along that stretch of highway and our driver refused to travel it until an all clear had been declared. When he felt it was safe, he drove as fast as he could through the dangerous zone. We on board were looking out the windows, trying to spot the "enemy." I felt anger mixed with fear as I knew that the weapons and ammunition being used by the Contras were manufactured in our country, and potentially could have been lethal to U.S. citizens on that bus. The resolution against U.S. policy passed with little opposition, though there was one comment that some present felt they had been emotionally manipulated by my presentation. So be it!

Tom continued serving the Presbytery of Chicago in its ministries among Hispanics. In 1984 he accepted a call to pastor the English congregation of the Ravenswood Presbyterian Church. This was a bilingual church, and he was privileged to serve together with Rev. Samuel Acosta, who shepherded the Hispanic members. My request for office space in the church, for the Central Midwest Witness for Peace work, was turned down, as WFP was considered too "political" for some of the members. I had been ordained as an elder in Lake View Presbyterian Church, so I chose to remain active in that small church. We were grateful to be able to continue to live with Grandma Gyori, at 3913 N. St. Louis, enabling both Tom and I to commute easily around the city, and to live very sustainably.

We needed only one car, as I, who didn't drive, could use Chicago's good public transit system.

Tom's ministry at Ravenswood was always challenging, but his excellent people skills and pastoral gifts enabled him to have a fulfilling ministry there. Rev. Magdalena Garcia followed don Samuel as the pastor of the Ravenswood Hispanic congregation. This is the church in which she had grown up. Before enrolling in McCormick Seminary, she had served as the clerk of session. Tom had married Magdalena and Augusto Torres earlier, and they were close personal friends as well as colleagues in ministry. Even though I remained a regular participant and member at Lake View, I became well acquainted with the wonderful people at Ravenswood.

One project we developed was a collaboration between Lake View and Ravenswood. We jointly planted the "Organic Faith Garden" on some of the extensive land surrounding the Ravenswood Church. With the enthusiastic help of many willing hands, the perimeters were defined, and a good-sized plot was tilled. Soon seedlings I had started were planted and we were on our way to experiencing the joys and challenges of community gardening. Tom and I spent many happy hours planting, weeding, and harvesting tasty vegetables from that garden, along with the various people from the churches and the neighborhood. Long lasting friendships resulted, especially with several volunteers from McCormick Seminary who joined in the fun. We kept the garden functioning well for some five years, or so, until Tom retired in 1997.

Instructions for Living a Life

Pay attention.
Be astonished.
Tell about it.

— Mary Oliver, poet

In trying to "pay attention," I've been reading my journals covering about 40 years. Yes, I've "been astonished" and am now "talking about it." Unfortunately, I find that much of my writing in 1983 and 1984 was very introspective, musings about scriptures I was reading, and trying to find guidance from them for my increasingly busy life. These were insightful "conversations with God." At the beginning of Lent in 1984, I wrote, "What has God promised that I can expect God to fulfill along my Lenten journey? Some of my stops will be: Witness for Peace meeting in Santa Cruz, California, and speaking engagements in Champaign/Urbana, Illinois, and Naples, Florida." It turned out to be just a "starter" for that period!

Returning to Chicago, I was engulfed in catching up with the backlog of responsibilities: orienting upcoming Witness for Peace delegations headed for Nicaragua, tending to other matters related to WFP, the Pledge of Resistance in Chicago, and with the Presbytery's Central American Task Force. There was also work with the Sanctuary Movement, and the session of Lake View Church. Amidst these were family and family concerns as well.

My stepmother, Dorothea, was seriously ill in Lancaster, Pennsylvania, so after Easter I travelled there to support Daddy and struggle with the physicians; I disagreed with their course of treatment. The escalating conflicts in Central

America were always on my mind, heightened by my growing mistrust of President Reagan and his overt support of the Contras against the Sandinista government in Nicaragua. Gloria Kinsler was leading an important delegation to Guatemala which was slated to participate in a nation-wide protest in front of the National Palace; I was praying for her. All in all, this was a time of major internal concerns and conflicts clamoring for my attention. I kept repeating, "Be still and know that I am God" which helped me find a modicum of peace amidst the conflicts. "This is God's world, not mine!"

I then had to return to Lancaster for Dorothea's funeral! Sonja's graduation from Goshen College was looming and Ken was not able to attend this milestone event; I was upset. During all this angst, Tom was the bulwark of gentle, loving support. I was feeling overwhelmed, convinced of my inadequacy as an organizer and of my inability to adequately fulfill my responsibilities. I wrote, "The Psalmists countered despair by praising God." With that came the assurance that I was doing my best to "tell about" the things which were so compelling in my life. "Praising God does work!" I concluded.

As the year of 1985 came to an end, I recorded some of the highlights. Tom's celebration of 25 years of ministry was eclipsed by Sonja and Ray's engagement. My intense involvement with the turmoil in Central America and my travels there and around the U.S. disengaged me from day to day family activities. Tom and I did squeeze in some regenerative trips together, one being ten days in New Mexico. We were welcomed by friends in that beautiful state who lived in Albuquerque and Las Vegas. Ken and Bea moved to Austin, Texas, where he enrolled in postgraduate studies. Sarah Elizabeth, born to Tom and Lisa and our first grandchild, made her appearance in Raleigh on November 6.

During that time, we bought the Ogle's cottage in Beverly Shores, Indiana. Son in law Ray and a buddy did a beautiful remodeling job on the house. Tom resigned from his staff position on the Presbytery staff as liaison with the Hispanic pastors in Chicago. Our entire extended family joined us in Chicago to celebrate Christmas, including my dad. As I wrote about these activities, a self-sustaining thread helped weave my life together in the form of regular meditation on scriptures and deepening relationships with supportive friends.

On February 4, 1988, prayers were answered when congress defeated President Reagan's insistence on further monetary aid to the Contras, still fighting in Nicaragua. How we had agonized, worked, prayed, and demonstrated in the hopes we could collectively influence our elected officials to vote for Life instead of Death. I had found much needed support in scripture passages and fasting and praying. Faith in our redemptive, loving God was indeed rewarded. Unfortunately, that one vote did not end U.S. military intervention in Central America, and our advocacy work had to continue.

In early 1989, I was feeling near burnout with trying to provide leadership on too many fronts. Before weaning myself away from my work with WFP, I led two almost back-to-back delegations through Central America, I found each to be challenging and fulfilling, reinforcing my sense of call and my ability to do this work.

The second delegation was one organized by Dr. Rosemary Reuther from Chicago. It was an honor to work with her and know of her personal commitment to human rights and justice in Central America, introducing her and her students to the ongoing realities of Central America was a joy-filled challenge. A highlight of this trip was visiting a newly established village in El Salvador now inhabited by people who had fled their homes during the height of the conflict in their country. They were a living sign of hope. They had escaped into neighboring Honduras where they lived for several years in U.N. operated refugee camps. They shared very graphically the stories of swimming across the Lempa River as planes overhead strafed them with bullets. Now they were rebuilding their shattered lives by establishing a vibrant, new community.

A Remarkably Restorative Vacation

Later that year, Tom and I packed our camping gear in a large duffle bag and flew to Seattle, Washington. There we found a bustling, growing, prosperous metropolis, which despite its impressive development, held little attraction for me. It quickly faded into memory upon our arrival at magnificent Mt. Rainier. Here is an excerpt from my journal of this joy-filled experience.

"Our camp site was graced with an icy, bubbling mountain creek, our hammocks secured to towering pines which roofed our tent. I have no words to describe the beauty we experienced as ever more awesome vistas came into view with every bend in the five-hour hike we took on Thursday. The boiling, crashing White River tumbled beside us at times. Then the trail led us through an enchanted forest. Soon we were awed by the sight of a huge glacier out of which gushed the river.

The final 168 steps led us to the climax of the trail, Glacier Basin, at the foot of Mt. Rainier. Open meadows, filled with dazzling wildflowers were ringed by brilliantly green evergreens. The snow fields of the mountain gleamed in the sun as a group of climbers began their ascent. Snow, dug out of a bank, refreshed us as we had not taken water with us. Hopefully, Tom's camera captured faithfully the incredible scene. The variety of delicate flowers were a constant source of wonder and inspiration.

"After a refreshing repast of chicken sandwiches at the campsite, we drove off to Paradise. This incredibly magnificent place is on the southern flanks of Mt. Rainier, as opposed to the northern exposure we had enjoyed earlier. Once again, every turn in the road exposed us to enthralling vistas of mountain ranges, rushing streams, deep gorges, all under the majestic watch of Mt. Rainier. The grand Paradise Inn provides hospitality that does justice to the glorious setting it rests in. Coffee and delicious apple cobbler were served to us in gracious style to cap off an unforgettable day."

The following days of this vacation took us to Butchart Gardens in British Columbia, another thrilling display of God's magnificent creation leading me to quote the Psalmist, "What are we, humans, that Thou art mindful of us?" We couldn't leave the great northwest without visiting my Uncle Will, in Everett, Washington. We spent a delightful evening with him in his home, listening to engaging stories of China. This is just a sampling of the memorable travels that enriched Tom and me, returning a semblance of balance into our overly busy lives back in Chicago.

CHAPTER 15

Nicaraguan Elections

> Say among the nations,
>   Our God reigns supreme!
> The world stands firm and unshakable:
>   Our God will judge each nation with strict justice
> **PSALM 90:10**

> Do not trust in rulers,
>   In mortals in whom there is no salvation.
> **PSALM 145:3.**

The Nicaraguan presidential elections were scheduled for February 1990, with Daniel Ortega the candidate for the Sandinista party and Violeta Chamorro the candidate for UNO, the opposition party. Witness for Peace was asked to be one of the international monitoring groups in designated polling stations around the country.

I was asked to lead a group of rather high-profile religious leaders who were warm, well organized, and flexible, making it a joy to be more supportive than directive in working with them. The WFP Nicaragua team did a masterful job of arranging many diverse interviews with people representing the different parties. We met with Christians in the base communities in various neighborhoods of Managua. Here we observed the careful instructions given to people about the logistics of voting and expectations of the general populace such as: no alcohol to be served on the day of elections, no campaigning after the prior Wednesday. A week prior to the elections was designated a week of prayer. Churches across the country were open all day Saturday for this purpose. Here are some notes from my journal, about election day.

"At 6 a.m. three of us walked to a near-by polling station to observe the setup and opening of the polls. With meticulous care and formality, the election personnel put in order each piece of equipment and all material that had been delivered. Here 370 people had registered, and they were given ballots for each of the three votes, president, national assembly and municipal officials. After assembling the voting booths and ballot boxes, the ballots were duly counted and observed by members of the opposition party, UNO and the FSLN, incumbents, and other official observers like ourselves."

We observed voting in about 36 precincts, after dividing into 6 groups during the day, we saw no incidents of irregularity. We were extremely impressed with the exemplary procedures as well as courteous comportment of all involved. One can only wish voting in our country would be as immaculate! We returned to Managua tired but expectant around 10 p.m.

Anne Worely woke me at 3:15 am saying things weren't going well, UNO was leading, and maintained the lead. Violeta Chamorro won by an astounding margin! We were devastated! Outgoing President Daniel Ortega gave a moving concession speech, carefully measuring each word, affirming the will of the people. The FSLN's goals were always to respect the collective voice of the Nicaraguan people as expressed at the polls.

Shock was felt all day Monday. Many analyses were shared including "low intensity war won the day." "Revolution in Latin America must never happen again against the U.S." seemed to be the messages. Much heart searching must be made about what took place on February 25, 1990, in Nicaragua.

This defeat of the Sandinistas is so much more profound than a political loss. How do we keep the dream alive? The symbol of hope that Nicaragua offered the world is deeply rooted. God has always worked with, punished, and re-established nations. How does one judge the activity of God with a given nation at a given moment in time? Confucius is quoted as saying "Our greatest glory is not in never falling, but in rising every time we fall.'" Rev. Gustavo Parajon encouraged us by reading from II Corinthians 4:1–17, which includes these words, "We are afflicted in every way possible, but we are not crushed; we are full of doubts, but never despair." I left Nicaragua filled with anguished questions.

Busy days in late spring were relieved by restful days spent in Loma Linda, which became my physical/spiritual retreat. In June, back to Guatemala for WFP business and the opportunity to be present to welcome Sonja and Ray as they began their term of service with the Mennonite Central Committee in Guatemala.

Poet Ted Loder's words were an encouragement and nourished my spent soul.

Eternal Friend, grant me an ease
to breathe deeply of this moment,
this light, this miracle of now.

Beneath the din and fury of great movements
and harsh news and urgent crises,
make me attentive still to good news
to small occasions
and the grace of what is possible
for me to be, to do, to give, to receive.

That I may miss neither my neighbor's gift
Nor my enemy's need.

CHAPTER 16

Israel/Palestine

Israel, put your hope in our God,
For with Adonai is abundant love
And the fullness of deliverance,
God will deliver Israel from all its failings.
PSALM 130:7,8

First, I need to state our opinion. We do not equate Judaism or Zionism, with the State of Israel. Criticism of the political State of Israel is entirely separate from anti-Semitism. We must remember that Palestinians are also Semites.

Here I recount another extraordinary trip Tom and I shared in 1990. We participated in a delegation to the Middle East, led by our good friend from the Covenant Community, Rev. Don Wagner. This experience took place shortly after Saddam Hussein had invaded Kuwait, thus tensions in the region were palpable. On August 15, we arrived in Amman Jordan, en route to Palestine/Israel. We were a group of 15 disparate people, ready and eager to embark on an adventure we had been preparing for under Don's capable tutelage, having read assigned pieces and trying to be open to what lay ahead.

Again, I quote from my journals: Sunday, August 20. "Today is our third day in Jerusalem, following a killer schedule, at least unrelenting! On Friday, we arrived after a long delay at the border due to the harassment of Don Wagner, whose name appeared on their computer. Following a sumptuous salad lunch, we listened to three Jews in the peace movement, representatives of the Women in Black who oppose Israeli occupation of the West Bank and Gaza. "It is very bad to be an occupier and a torturer", they commented.

Our walking tour of Old Jerusalem elicited in me all kinds of unexpected feelings. All shops were closed because of the Palestinian strikes, so the streets were virtually empty. Our guide impressed on me the ancient history of Christianity and the various Orthodox expressions and traditions. The Church of the Holy Sepulcher is considered sacred space by conflictive traditions. It was filled with tourists which erased any sacred sense for me, leaving no aura of anything awesome or holy.

Then we were shown the recent Jewish occupation of St. John's Hospice, a Palestinian Christian place, which seemed to highlight the hopelessly entangled conflict between Israel and Palestine. Next, a woman working for Al-Haq, a Palestinian human rights documentation/investigative center, gave us another thought-provoking presentation. She impressed me with the quality of the work they do, reporting a 70% success rate of cases investigated in Ramallah.

In Bethlehem, in one hour while we were in Manger Square, we observed the capture of at least three Palestinian youth (one was 8 yrs. old) by Israeli military. This incident has occupied much group time and discussion. We ultimately wrote several affidavits under the direction of an American Civil Liberties Union (ACLU) attorney. Several visceral feelings have been aroused. Soldiers are victims as well as the three youths. Children were being mistreated by soldiers. A hysterical mother was frantically seeking help.

Our next stop was the Bethlehem Bible College where we talked with three evangelical Christian Palestinians. One was a graduate of Fuller Seminary and the other was from the Mennonite Biblical Seminary in Elkhart, Indiana. I was surprised at their adamant criticism of the Israeli government and their clear biblical critique of the Jewish State. "We Palestinians are also to be recipients of God's promises to Abraham, whose seed produced both Arabs and Jews," they said. Their explanation of the Israeli settlements was clear: 1) Much of the land being settled by them was not held by individual title-holders but was owned communally for grazing by Palestinians since time immemorial. 2) Land which has not been cultivated for a given period can be confiscated by the Israeli government. 3) Settlers drill deep wells, lowering the water table for adjoining Palestinian land, and Israel won't give permits to Palestinians to drill new wells. 4)The lack of water is forcing some Palestinians off their land. We were also informed about the Christian Embassy, a Christian Zionist, fundamentalist group we are hearing more and more about.

At the Evangelical Boys' Home, a clergyman said what we have heard repeated so often, "If it is so wrong for Iraq to occupy Kuwait, why is it o.k. for Israel to occupy Palestine?" He reminded us of how different Israeli leaders have referred to Palestinians as "cockroaches," "grasshoppers," and other insults. His voice was one among many Christians we talked with who called upon U.S. Christians to stand up and oppose Israeli injustices in Palestine.

In Bet Zahur, on Saturday, August 19, we met some inspiring young professionals. They personified the heart and head of the Intifada, being the strategists and analysts of the movement who are "shaking off" the Israeli occupation by civil disobedience and confronting the Israeli war machine directly and courageously. The Intifada began in a refugee camp in Gaza, but quickly spread to the West Bank. These professionals explained their civil disobedience as not paying taxes and using the strike strategy. Palestinian shops close every afternoon at 1:30. Income is reduced but so is spending. People have extra time for organizing, education, and relationship building among neighbors.

Later, our interview with Bob Lang at the Jewish settlement, Ephrata, gave us a good picture of how Jews feel about their "right" to occupy land in Palestine. A religious political arrogance seems to motivate them. A rabbi told us, "Jerusalem is the soul of the Jews, therefore must not be divided." "Jews have a biblically mandated right to 27,000 square kilometers of territory—the Jewish State. Arabs have 20 countries they can live in; the Palestinians can go to Jordan."

The Yad va Shem Holocaust Martyrs and Heroes Museum was a dramatic reminder of human barbarity and tragic suffering. Several of us were struck with the comparisons of those days and today. I was impressed by the trees that were planted on both sides of the walkway, each one commemorating non-Jews who had sheltered and protected Jews from the Nazis. I want to be counted among the "trees planted by the streams of living water," providing protection and help for people endangered by human evil, especially Central Americans, but also Palestinians. I think of Psalm 1.

Phil Wilcox, the Consul General, received us in the cool, beautiful garden of the U.S. Consulate in Jerusalem. He is a self-confident, knowledgeable diplomat. He commented that it is not helpful to compare Germany's treatment of the Jews with today's Israeli treatment of Palestinians.

We found his Beatitude Michael Sabbath, Latin Patriarch, to be very formal, not a very engaging presenter. He reiterated many things we had heard. He stressed that the Israeli occupation of St John's Hospice on Maundy Thursday this year is being challenged in courts, but not moving very fast. Rt. Rev. Semir Kafity, bishop of the Anglican Church, was more friendly. He is the pastor of St. George's Cathedral. He stressed the criticism of Israeli actions as a matter of human rights violations, not anti-Semitism. "I wish the U.S. would use spiritual (moral), not capitalist motivations for setting economic policies for the world." Like so many others, he condemned Iraq's invasion of Kuwait, even though the boundaries between the two are artificial. He also condemned more U.S. military actions in Saudi Arabia. He continued by saying, "Israel has never defined its borders and let Palestine live securely in the 23% of the land as was required by the U.N." He, like the men at the Bethlehem Bible College, referred to Christian fundamentalists' alliance with fanatical Zionism, the Christian Embassy, and the Christian Broadcasting Network, etc. as distorting the reality of Israel/Palestine.

The following day in Nazareth, we met Anglican Archdeacon Ria Abu Al-Assal. "I am an Arab Palestinian, Anglican Christian, and Israeli," he declared. "We have been here since the first Pentecost. Living stones, not ancient stones of 'holy places,' we are the important ones.. We Arab Christians have lost the past (in 700 A.D. 75% 'drifted away,' many becoming Muslims). We must not lose the present and therefore the future." He is trying to create an authentically Arab Christian theology and liturgy.

Rev. Elias Chacour had a profound impact on me. "Men and women are all created in God's image; we are only one race, one people, chosen and beloved," he said. He reflected on a common theme articulated broadly in Israel: "A land with no people for a people with no land." "We must re-humanize each other, not treat Jews like dirt, as did the Nazis, nor treat Palestinians as such. Jews are jeopardizing Israel's existence by their inhumane actions against the Palestinians. We are separated by walls of hate, bitterness and fear, not of stones." Father Chacour sees much hope in the gains of the Intifada, including a new way of relating, basically a nonviolent movement, and helping Jews and peace groups relate to people in the West Bank.

On to Tel Aviv via Galilee and Tiberias. Tel Aviv is a bustling, burgeoning, modern metropolis on the shores of the Mediterranean. We enjoyed a marvelously refreshing swim in the sea, which was all too brief. This drive was such a pleasant contrast to the arid desert through which we had been traveling up to this point. We passed many lovely olive groves and other green agriculture. Unfortunately, we were unable to swim in the Sea of Galilee but did make a stop at the Jordan River. There were many pictures taken and many people collected some water to take home.

The only time I felt a sense of the "holy" or "biblical nostalgia," was on the Mount of Beatitudes where we stopped and had a group reflection. The steps we sat upon are part of a Franciscan Monastery or retreat center and is a lovely spot overlooking the Sea of Galilee.

Chaim Shur, editor of the New Outlook Magazine, offered a few rays of hope for me. He mentioned planning a series of public seminars to discuss concerns between Jews and Palestinians. He affirmed a two-state solution as the only viable response to the conflict. "This land must be recognized by all as the joint homeland of both people", he said. Chaim's comments about the Israeli economy and the massive influx of Soviet Jews were enlightening. How to accommodate the Soviets remained a question. I was impressed with his comment that, in order for opposing factions to find peace they must negotiate with their enemy, not with self-chosen representatives.

The office of Israel's Labor Party, with the posted schedule of meetings, with representatives from around the world, was impressive! Israel does have incredible influence and effective relationships internationally. Mr. Gat, the Labor representative, was an articulate proponent of a more moderate two-state solution. He expressed Israeli defense concerns, not just against Palestinians but all Arabs. Palestinians must be linked with Jordan in a federation. He recognized that the Palestinian refugees are a major problem. He seems to propose moving them to Jordan. He felt that the settlements might be dismantled. "We can overcome this problem of reintegrating settlers back into Israel." Don Wagner recognized nuances, which escaped most of the rest of us and called this man to task on several points. Don even exacted some concessions from Mr. Gat.

We left Tel Aviv and headed south to Gaza. The driver seemed quite happy to deposit us at the military check point. Don was glad to see the Near East Council of Churches' vans waiting for us. Because of the sensitivity of the area, we designated Susan to be our "official" photographer. She went crazy shooting pictures rapid fire the whole time we were in Gaza! The place was bristling with Israeli military; clearly this was an occupied territory.

We were warmly welcomed at the Marna House in Gaza City. It is a simple but comfortable large house which provides hospitality for foreign documentary film crews, as well as the likes of us. They have a growing video library of tapes, taken by visitors and donated to Marna House. These are available for viewing by guests. We saw one which was very well done. It focused on an Indian doctor who worked in the local clinic or hospital. She was very articulate in explaining how children were treated by the Israeli forces. The video also had clips with interviews of young Israeli soldiers who admitted dislike for having to apprehend children. They must follow orders, however. Someone told us that the special forces deployed to Gaza were carefully selected, being young men and those who had experienced some violence, either personally or to members of their families at the hands of Palestinians.

Mrs. Usra el Barberi, over 70 years old and born in Gaza, impressed us all with her presentation on the porch of Marna House. She was the first Palestinian woman to receive a university education, at the University of Cairo. She has been refused an exit permit to travel abroad. She has been invited to speak at any number of international events. She is perceived as a threat to Israeli security. Physically, no, but certainly as a prophetess and articulate spokeswoman for the Palestinians!

One issue that came up several times was that of collective punishment. If a child was apprehended for rock throwing, the entire family could be evicted from their home and the house razed. They are also fined from $500–$2,500 and more commonly now set at 4–5,000 shekels.

Mohammad Abu-Shaban, a Palestinian lawyer in Gaza, led a hunger strike from May 22–27, 1990, as a nonviolent protest to the occupation and curfews, He shared the deep anger and frustration of the Palestinians by quoting a client, "I see soldiers chasing and killing children every day. I see them breaking kids' bones right in front of me." Apparently the soldiers agree on what part of the body to attack on a given day. Sometimes it's the legs, other times, the face or the kidneys. Mohammad has had only one or two victories out of the 1,805 cases he has defended in the courts!

"How do I sort this all out? What are the major themes to develop and share with people who have understood little more than I have," I asked myself? To do so, I began to organize my experiences around the following five themes:

(1) Current Israeli/Palestinian situation with brief history of settlements, Zionism, human rights violations.
(2) Israeli peace movement
(3) Intifada
(4) Christians in Israel
(5) Opinions on current crisis

We returned to Jordan where we met the director general of the Middle East Council of Churches, a Palestinian, who was an agitated man as he spoke with us. "All we Palestinians are asking for is a third of our land," he explained. There have been about 242 resolutions regarding Palestine before the U.N. The U.S. has vetoed more than 200. He repeated what we had heard many times, "Security cannot be established by force, but by peace." Another recurring theme was the U.S.'s double standards in foreign policy and regarding human rights. Why not condemn Israeli invasion of Lebanon, the West Bank, and Gaza, Syria's invasion of Lebanon? The U.N. Resolution 24.2 which calls for Israeli withdrawal from the Occupied Territories, is important, and again was referred to several times. The State of Palestine has been recognized by more than 100 countries, more than have recognized the State of Israel!

Our meeting with the Palestinian National Council (PNC) in Jordan was a fascinating experience. They are the Palestinian government in exile. Their leader received all kinds of deference by the three other members of the PNC who met with us. He said he doesn't like seeing U.S. troops supporting corrupt sheiks and national leaders as in Saudi Arabia, where King Fahd is "the biggest gambler in the world!" he claimed. "The U.S. is recognizing the least democratic regimes in the region," he said. This interview brought an end to this unforgettable experience for Tom and me. It expanded our commitment to advocate for the human rights of not just Central Americans, but now also for Palestinians.

As a result of what we learned in Palestine/Israel, we initiated seminars and conversations, specifically in Lake View Presbyterian Church in Chicago. Three young women responded dramatically to these presentations by joining the Christian Peacemakers Teams (CPT) working in the Middle East. Separately, all three went to Palestine on CPT delegations. One returned to work effectively, both locally in the Presbytery of Chicago and with the national church, advocating for changes in U.S. policies toward the region. Another ended up spending several years in northern Iraq during the war, also with CPT.

These many years later, I continue to receive updates on this beleaguered region through CPT, the Presbyterian Church, and the Churches for Middle East Peace. The sad truth remains that little has changed in Israel's apartheid treatment of the Palestinians, including now the erection of the tortuous wall, further dividing Jews from Palestinians, as well as Palestinians from their cultivated lands, Palestinian children from access to schools, and rough treatment at check points.

The ongoing plight of the Palestinians remains a major concern of mine now in 2022. I try to keep updated and for anyone who wants to have current information, especially about the decline of a Christian presence in Israel/Palestine, I refer you to the excellent reporting of the Churches for The Middle East, info@cmep.org. Also I find Sabeel, a Middle East liberation theology center provides thoughtful analysis of the region. Read about their work, sabeel@sabeel.org We know so little of the impact of Israeli settlements in the West Bank, Zionism, and human rights violations. The realities of life in the Gaza strip are absolutely appalling and have been recently detailed by Jonathan Gottlieb from Sabeel.

CHAPTER 17

Quiet Retreat

Be still and know that I am God!
I will be exalted among the nations;
I will be exalted upon the earth.

PSALM 46:10

Stillness was the least of all the feelings engulfing me at the beginning of 1991! The thunderous roar of war sounded loud and clear, both within and without. I had designated at least the month of February as a time for a silent retreat at Loma Linda, a time of renewal and discernment about my personal future. At the same time, President George W. Bush and his government were deciding whether to declare war on Iraq because of their dislike of its president, Saddam Hussein. The U.S. had invested heavily in upgrading our war machine with the latest technology, awaiting testing in a war theatre. The arms industry was clearly beating the drums for such a declaration. Ironically, Bush set the deadline for the decision to fall on January 15, Martin Luther King's birthday memorial! The next day, January 16, war was declared. all hell broke out, and we are still engulfed in the consequences of those decisions

20 years later! How could I responsibly "retreat" into solitude at such a moment?

Fortunately, the inner voice prevailed, and I pressed ahead with my plans for a two month sabbatical, alone, midwinter, at Loma Linda. February 1, through Easter were the dates I had set. With meditation and books in hand, Tom left me alone in my favorite "house of prayer."

All of my inner resources were spent! In the six weeks leading up to February 1, I had helped orient a Witness for Peace delegation headed for Guatemala and Nicaragua, in Miami. That was followed by a WFP regional gathering at Loma Linda, then on to Washington, D.C., for a national gathering of WFP, where my sabbatical plan was warmly encouraged by many good friends in attendance. Back in Chicago I helped organize a retreat of the Chicago Religious Task Force on Central America, which was an energizing event. At Lake View Church, our Church and Society Committee convened for planning our response to this declaration of war. On January 17, I joined the protest march winding its way through downtown Chicago, several thousand people participating! Finally, I accepted the invitation to make a presentation on Guatemala to a group on the South Side of Chicago; Tom accompanied me. Following this he drove me out to Loma Linda. I was ready to retreat!

Sabbatical

O God, create a clean heart in me,
Put into me a new and steadfast spirit.
PSALM 51: 10

The soil of my soul was depleted, parched, and unproductive, desperately in need of tilling, watering, and composting. Little growth could be expected without major renewal. How could any new seeds of vision stand a chance of germinating, or sprouting, much less ripening, into nourishing fruit without major cultivation? That was the state of my being as I entered into this three-month sabbatical in February of 1991. Having been a vegetable gardener most of my adult life, I was aware of the disciplined planning and anticipated hard work it takes to cultivate a productive garden. I embarked on a carefully designed plan of action of how to structure the upcoming time away from my hectic life, uninterrupted by calls to action, travel, and the energy-draining activities of the past years.

"Love lures new patterns of creation out of the void," guided my efforts to rejuvenate the soil of my soul. These included rest, renewal, meditation practices, creative projects, and exercise. In fact, new patterns emerged as I learned to bask in God's love, absorb the healing waters and be calmed by the gentle winds of the Spirit. So much to learn about being "still," and even more about "knowing God is God."

Gratefully, the combined resources of scripture, books and prayer during long walks on the beach, even in the cold, wintery, February days, brought forgiveness and clarity and small signs of new growth and life.

I find in my journal, written during this intensely healing time, helpful insights into how to live in today's complexities which demand love, faith and action. My anger flares as I perceive the deafening silence of prophetic voices from churches and others of faith, which seems to add to the apparent apathy of the general public. Why is it so difficult to speak truth to power? What are we afraid of? Fortunately, today I'm hearing voices raised against the egregious racist, misogynistic, cruel policies being put forth by the Trump administration. God-fearing leaders and the voices of young people are demanding attention to the catastrophic climate disasters falling upon our one earth. May we have the courage, wisdom, and compassion to join them!

My less than healthy relationships with Tom, his mom, and my sister Rosaline, absorbed much prayer and pondering, which did lead to some resolutions, for which I was grateful. Painful weeding began to bear fruit. Most rewarding was my ability to discuss all of this openly with Tom, which deepened our love and commitment. Rosaline spent a few days with me during this time, and I was disappointed in a less than satisfactory sharing with her about what I was learning and enjoying during this sabbatical.

Arriving at Holy Week, I needed to return to family life, renewed and enthusiastic to follow God's leading in the days to come. My soul was replenished; many new seeds sown had begun to flourish, and the promise of new life was exciting. As in the life of any garden, there were many fallow, dry and seemingly unproductive days during the rest of that year. Personal reflection and introspection absorbed me in my ongoing struggle to discern new guidance for my life.

CHAPTER 18

Goodbye Daddy

Adonai, you have been our refuge
  From one generation to the next.
Before the mountains were born,
    You brought forth the earth and the world,
    You are God without beginning or end.
You turn humankind back into dust
    And say. "Go back, creatures of the earth!"
For in your sight a thousand years
    Are like yesterday, come and gone,
    No more than a watch in the night.
You sweep us away like a dream,
    Fleeting as the grass that springs up in the morning
    —
In the morning it sprouts,
But by evening it has withered and died.

PSALM 90:1–6

On Saturday, April 25, 1992, Arthur Bramwell Allen died. Rosaline and her girls had spent Easter with him the week before and had returned to Windsor, Ontario. Tom and I then drove to Lancaster to take up the vigil at his bedside in the hospital, then Tom returned home. I had stepped out of his room on that Saturday noon. I returned to find Daddy had breathed his last while I was out. In my grief, I hugged the attending nurse, as I was filled with remorse for my absence. Tom did a masterful job of leading the funeral service at Lammamuir House, Daddy's last place of residence. We were so grateful for the loving care we all received during this time of final farewell. Most of our family joined us in this celebration of Arthur Allen's memorably faithful and well-lived life. Grieving his departure absorbed many subsequent days for me.

On Daddy's 90th birthday, celebrated in Raleigh, we had presented him with a beautifully calligraphed picture of this song we had written together, then sang it to him to the tune of one of his favorite hymns, "Finlandia." The last stanza reads:

God's given you ninety years of joy-filled life,
And a heritage of which you can be proud.

You've shared God's word wherever you have lived
Challenging friends and family alike.

We celebrate your life, your gifts, your love,
God says to you, "Well done my son, well done!"

CHAPTER 19

Homecoming or Going?

Now set our captive hearts free, Adonai!
Make them like streams in the driest desert!
Then those who now sow in tears
  Will reap with shouts of joy
  Those who go out weeping as they
  Carry their seed for sowing,
  Will come back with shouts of joy
  As they carry their harvest home.

PSALM 126:4–6

On January 20, 1993, a modern-day exodus began for 2480 Guatemalan refugees who had been living in exile in Mexico for over a decade, under the auspices of the United Nations. A dramatic, hopeful change had begun. Sixty-eight buses accompanied by a number of service vehicles, including those carrying animals belonging to the returnees, made up a caravan stretching several kilometers in length.

I accompanied returnees on bus #4. Emotions were mixed as we crossed the border at La Mesilla, Guatemala. Most had not been inside their home country for up to 12 years. Tears of joy mixed with apprehension coursed down our cheeks as we were welcomed by hundreds of fellow country people, waving flags, exploding firecrackers and playing marimbas. My seat mate was 5 year old Bernardo. He was fascinated and bewildered by all the excitement: motorcycle cops, helicopters flying overhead photographing the events, and the crowds of people greeting us.

One can only imagine the logistical challenges of feeding, housing, and providing "pit stops" for close to 3,000 people as we wended our way down the Pan American Highway to Guatemala City and beyond! These tasks had been relegated to different organizations: U.N., government agencies, and the Catholic church, to name a few. The very capable organizers of the refugees had articulated their conditions for the return. These included the right to a voluntary, organized return, the right to associate and travel freely once inside their country, the right to land, to international accompaniment and most basic of all, the right to life and "physical integrity." Needless to say, this took careful, extended negotiating with all parties involved, but the returnees won the day.

Nobel prize winner, Rigoberta Menchu, travelled with us to Guatemala City and at each stop she gave us a message of encouragement. She inspired the refugees not to flag in their determination to work together with fellow citizens to bring freedom, dignity and peaceful change to this war torn nation.

For two weeks, I rode, slept and ate with Bernardo and the other 37 people on bus #4. Together, we enjoyed the huge welcoming parties and religious events in Huehuetenango, Chimaltenango, Guatemala City and, finally, in Coban. Our daughter, Sonja and her family were living along the highway, near Chimaltenango, so I abandoned ship for one night. Shortly after having arrived in their home, we boarded their pick-up truck and drove to the edge of the highway to join residents in greeting the rest of the caravan. Three year old Erin was overjoyed at being allowed to honk the truck's horn as many times as she wished! How I reveled in taking a hot shower and playing with our two grandchildren, Erin and James, during my one night stay with them. The following day they drove me in to Guatemala City where I rejoined my friends from bus #4. We had been assigned to stay in a Catholic church, sleeping on the pews.

Wearily, we left the buses in Coban at the end of long days of travel. We shivered together in the chilling rain and many of us succumbed to colds, sharing in the dramatic changes the returnees were experiencing. We were housed in a convent where sisters lovingly passed through the crowds, offering welcome, first aid, food, and space to spread out our sleeping gear. I made several trips to the market with returnees, helping them obtain warm clothing, shoes, and other necessities.

With sadness, on January 29, I left my "'extended family" in Coban. My exhaustion and cold had developed to the point I could not continue with them. I was aware that the hardest part of their journey still lay ahead aboard huge dump trucks. Two and a half days of grueling travel were yet to be traversed. Because of the rain, the roads became all but impassable, resulting in the U.N. agreeing to fly all women with children under ten and other vulnerable people to the destination in the middle of the jungle in the Ixcan.

Skepticism runs deep about the commitment of the Guatemalan government to ensure peace and even a modicum of security for all people in their country to this day. Conflict resolution skills were engaged in the months that followed, as returnees negotiated new living and farming spaces in villages from which they had fled. Former family and friends who had stayed during the dangerous days of civil war were not always welcoming to those who had fled to Mexico, where many had improved their lives, now asking to be able to live in houses inhabited by others and to farmlands now being tended by former friends.

In subsequent years, I visited two communities of those returned refugees, to find vibrant, flourishing communities, proudly displaying new life and purpose. The first was in Xaman, Coban, and the second one was in Nueva Esperanza in Huehuetenango. Martha Pierce, a good friend from Evanston, Illinois, accompanied those from Mexico who returned to an empty field in 1994. Nueva Esperanza has been developed into a thriving community with paved streets, substantial homes and bustling businesses. Martha has led delegations to this town every year since their return. They enjoy the festivities celebrating that momentous event of more than 25 years ago.

CHAPTER 20

Xaman, Coban, Guatemala

O n January 23, 1996, I returned to Guatemala. This time I joined a delegation organized by my friends, Paula Bidle, Martha Pierce and Linda McCrae, sponsored by the United Church of Christ. This was one delegation for which I had no leadership responsibility, leaving me free to enjoy the experience in a much more relaxed way. We visited "La Isla" a community on the outskirts of Guatemala City which has an ongoing relationship with a Lutheran congregation in Fargo, North Dakota. I was duly impressed with what seemed to be an exemplary relationship between a U.S. congregation and a Guatemalan faith community.

After a couple of days, we boarded a bus to Coban, from where we would continue to Xaman, the home of Guatemalan refugees who had returned to their home country in 1995. We rode standing in the back of a truck for 12 hours over a rocky road, plowing through incredible mud holes, some six feet deep. We arrived bone tired, tied up our hammocks in the church and retired without delay.

The community of Xaman is spread across a wide tract of land which was divided into three barrios. The first one accommodated people who had not fled to Mexico but had remained in the area. Others, from the Kekchi tribe, were returnees who had been originally sent to "Victoria 20" farther north. People from the Kanjobal tribe settled in the second barrio, and the third housed Mam Indigenous people. In a little over a year, these enterprising people had built a church, a school, a medical clinic, and housing for doctors from Doctors Without Borders, in addition to each family's individual house. A well organized and functioning community had evolved, and we were privileged to meet with representatives of each barrio who shared with us their hopes and dreams going forward.

Linda McCrae led us in some fascinating group dynamics, discussions and bible studies. Jose Maria Grave, a returnee, shared his story. Referring to the scripture passage in 1 Corinthians 12:12 about the body of Christ, he told us, "I feel like my body will never be complete. Since my wife died, I feel like I lost my right arm. God made us to live together in twos." He continued to recount how he and his wife had had long discussions about whether to return to Guatemala or not. She was adamant saying, "We must return, even if it costs us our lives." Tragically, she had been killed the previous October during a massacre in Xaman.

Some of us gathered one afternoon at the local river to bathe and wash some clothes. Using a boot belonging to one of our members, we were able to rinse soap out of our hair and emerge thoroughly refreshed.

Our three days in this remarkable community exposed us to the resiliency, creativity, and cohesion of disparate people committed to making a new life amidst challenging conditions. We returned to Guatemala City renewed and profoundly impacted by the people with whom we had spent such quality time.

TRAUMATIC TRANSITIONS

Witness For Peace involvement winding down,
Regional leadership passed on,
Fewer delegations to the region,
Diminishing expertise on Central America,
These left me bereft of purpose. What now?

Restorative personal retreats to Loma Linda,
Leadership responsibilities at Lake View Church,
Counseling Central American refugees in Chicago,
Participation in Sanctuary Movement,
Kept me busy, but unfulfilled.

Growing tensions expressed in anger
At Mom Gyori and Tom,
Contradicted by affirmations of wisdom and leadership,
Created schizophrenic responses in me.

A sense of call eluded me.

CHAPTER 21

More Travels:
Hungary, England, and Turkey

May 7, 1995, at 5:30 p.m., British Airways carried sister Rosaline, Tom and me from Chicago to Budapest. Son Ken, Bea and Paul met us, and we settled into our quarters for the next few days. Having honed his tour guide expertise, Ken led us on local trams, trains, and buses to explore the wonders of Hungary's capital. Among the first was a memorable dip in their famous hot baths. Somehow Rosaline, Bea and I were separated from the men and led into a women's bath, requiring no bathing suits. To our embarrassment, we were given three skimpy 'aprons' as covering. We slinked awkwardly up a stairway to reach the pool. There we had to discard our 'aprons' and plunge naked into the pool and swim with local women, without the ability to communicate. When we finally returned to decent coverings and met the menfolk, we discovered they had enjoyed swimming in a co-ed pool with everyone wearing proper suits. This has become another humorous story to add to our family lore.

An evening cruise on the Danube River, visits to museums, markets, churches, and the Plaza of Heroes, filled our weekend with memorable moments.

On Saturday, Cousin Grace and her husband Maurice met us at Heathrow airport in London. Thus began a carefully choreographed visit among first cousins in England. Grace turned out to be a tiny, energetic, gracious and thoughtful hostess, accompanied by Maurice, a meticulous and kind man. Meeting for the first time, three of Grace's siblings who live in Kent, proved to be both fun and enlightening. Our emotional and informative conversations explained many feelings related to shared experiences with the China Inland Mission (CIM). Their parents, like ours, had been rejected by the CIM when they applied to return to China after a furlough. Bitterness remained among them because their parents were unable to support their six children in England, and some were placed temporarily in an orphanage. Also, they commented on how they felt that the Mission was dominated by upper class British elite and their values, thus explaining the insistence on British educational boarding schools like the one in Chefoo. All of this helps explain my feelings of abandonment by my parents during childhood.

Carefully planned tours of London, Cambridge, Birmingham and finally to Charborough, home of our grandfather, introduced me to much of my heritage. All too soon we boarded another plane, this time for Turkey. Why Turkey? Paul, Bea and Ken lived there and had for six years. Bea had prepared a sumptuous meal for us, and Paul was ecstatic about seeing us again!

Ken took us to Cappadocia straight away. Troglodyte rock formed spectacular surrealistic rock cones, capped pinnacles and fretted ravines, containing ancient catacombs and current residences. The five-star hotel in which we stayed was hewn out of this rock. Ken drove us out into the surrounding countryside for some awe-inspiring exploration of these fantastic structures, including a chapel with Christian symbols engraved on the walls.

We returned to our hotel and the most extravagant meal I have ever eaten! Several rooms were filled with tables. These were laden with hot and cold Turkish fare, an enormous choice of salads, entrees, desserts and finally a table loaded with fresh fruits, cheese and yogurt. Thirty dollars covered the total cost of this meal, our room and breakfast!

Returning to Ankara, we met many friends of Bea and Ken, did some sight-seeing, then flew to Ismir and drove along the coast to Ephesus. Continuing along the coast, we enjoyed swimming, snorkeling, and boating, spending a couple of nights in luxurious hotels. Upon flying to Istanbul, we stayed in a hotel facing the Blue Mosque, which was beautifully illuminated at night. St. Sophia's is a magnificent building, previously a church, then a mosque, and now a museum. A former Sultan's palace surrounded by lovely rose gardens and several buildings with blue tiled walls faced the Bospherus Channel. An important stop was a covered bazaar selling everything imaginable, including Turkish rugs. We crossed the channel to the Asian side of Istanbul, for a truly exotic fish dinner. I fell into bed exhausted after such a full day! Istanbul, a city of 12 million people, is full of amazing history and architecture which deserves weeks of exploration. We were impressed with Ken's grasp of interesting information and so many details. We flew out of Istanbul heading for home, filled with memories and emotions too numerous to unravel for days to come.

Southwest Fix

August 20, 1995, found us packing up our VW "Dreamcatcher" for a Southwest fix at Ghost Ranch, near Abiquiu, New Mexico. A radical change renewed our spirits. We reunited with old friends and enjoyed inspirational hiking among the stunning rock formations.

As I reflected on that spring and summer, I was most grateful as I recalled how our souls had feasted on God's remarkable displays of beauty. Among them were King's College Chapel in London, cliff dwellings in Cappadocia, rainbow-hued needle work in Budapest, happy smiles of grandchildren in Turkey and Chicago, and breathtaking scenes in New Mexico and Colorado. Finally, Tom and I celebrated 38 years of life together reveling at Claude Monet's spectacular paintings of the Art Museum in Chicago.

1998 began with Tom joining Martha Pierce for her annual delegation to Nueva Esperanza, Huehuetenango, Guatemala. Martha had accompanied Guatemalan refugees from Chiapas, Mexico, back home to Guatemala in 1995. At that time, they found the empty field which had been designated by the government for their establishing a new community. In celebration of that "homecoming", Martha has taken a small delegation of people from the U.S. to Nueva Esperanza every year for 25 years without interruption. She has watched that barren field develop into a thriving village, today replete with paved streets and even traffic lights! It was a different kind of experience for Tom to return to Guatemala without being directly motivated by Presbyterian Church related business. Nevertheless, he took full advantage of visiting old friends and places while there. He enjoyed sharing details of that experience with me upon his return. A few years later, I followed in his footsteps, joining another of Martha's delegations to Nueva Esperanza.

CHAPTER 22

Retirement to New Home

Thou who has brought us thus far on the way,
Thou who has by Thy might led us into the light,
Keep us forever in the path, we pray.
— JAMES WELDON JOHNSON,
IN "LIFT EVERY VOICE AND SING" (1900)

In March, Tom and I began the exciting, exhausting, almost daunting task of planning and executing the renovation of Loma Linda. Bob Hutchins, an architect and friend from Lake View Church, kindly drew up unofficial plans for the remake of this small, one bedroom home. Ray added his practical ideas to ensure the viability of the work ahead.

In late August, we organized at least two weekends in which we invited friends from Chicago to engage in our "demolition derbies" at Loma Linda. Folks came with pickaxes and sledgehammers to remove dry wall, a former deck, and to store furniture in the attic and basement. We paved the way for Doug Goetz, the contractor we had hired. We were blessed with lovely summer weather, affording us the luxury of refreshing swims in Lake Michigan at the end or these physically taxing days. We enjoyed working, playing and eating together with so many good friends.

It was fun making the choices of kitchen appliances, colors of paint for each room, a new insert for the fireplace, flooring, and the innumerable details of rehabbing an older building. It was a first for Tom and me, as this was the first property we had ever owned. We had been warned not to set our hearts on the termination date of Oct. 24, as stipulated in our contract with Doug. Indeed, our patience was tried more than once when he did no show up, sometimes for days at a time. Also, work was hampered by a powerful windstorm which felled a 70 foot willow tree across the path up to the house. In spite of frustrations which are to be expected during such projects, when all was said and done, we were pleased with the developing completion of our dreams for life in Loma Linda.

Saturday, Nov. 21, was moving day! Again, with the help of friends and family, we moved from 3913 N. St. Louis in Chicago to Loma Linda in Beverly Shores, Indiana. On Dec. 6, I spent my first day alone in our lovely new home with clothes in place in the closet, and plants distributed in chosen places. "I'm exhausted, burned out, planned out and unpacked out. Time to STOP!"

Many other activities added complexity to our lives during the reconstruction of our new home. We enjoyed various visits from members of our family; Tom went to Cuba in April, and I had impactful experiences in Chiapas.

In June, Mexico City was the site of the orientation of the board of directors of SIPAZ (Servicio Internacional de Paz), of which I was a member. Rev. Samuel Lobato challenged us. "Why in the world would SIPAZ venture into the murky world of ecumenical relations [in Chiapas]?" he asked. He continued by asserting that Mexican religious leaders each have their own agendas, which can be very difficult for foreigners to understand. Since I was asked by the board to help guide SIPAZ in ecumenical affairs, I felt most inadequate. Equally as discomforting for me was to be working again with people deeply committed to nonviolence while being in a place embroiled in violence. During my almost ten years of working with veteran pacifists with Witness for Peace in war torn Nicaragua, I should have felt self-confident working with the members of SIPAZ, persons equally engaged with alternatives to violence.

This time in Chiapas, we were privileged to learn from people at the Baptist Seminary, Bishop Samuel Ruiz, as well as local religious leaders from across the state. Our visit to Acteal was profoundly moving as we listened to first-hand accounts of the recent massacre which had taken place in their village. This community was a base for "Las Abejas," or "bees," a group of Catholics who believed in nonviolently working against the government. I scooped up some soil from the "holy ground" near the church where witnesses recounted the shock of losing family members to the attackers. Then, we ventured into Zapatista zones. There we learned from their leaders, who had taken up arms in opposition to the Mexican government's attempts to restrict land ownership by the native people who had lived on the land for generations. They had created designated zones of operation where they were forming alternative governance. Finally, we met with the mayor of Chenalho, who was a member of the national governing party, PRI. I journaled that "my body and brain were exhausted" after listening to so many conflicting commentaries of life lived in Chiapas, Mexico. I was ready to return home to renew plans and work on Loma Linda.

Preparing a Garden

Shrapnel recovered from Jalapa, Nicaragua, in 1983,
Soil removed from Acteal, Chiapas, in 1998,
uncovered during packing for our move to Loma Linda,
became brackets of my experiences with war
in Central America.

Books, papers, maps, and journals,
Sanctuary, Pledge of Resistance,
Witness for Peace, SIPAZ
Were the sum and substance defining
the garden of my life during those fifteen years.

These papers are buried at the entrance to Loma Linda,
Forming the base of a future garden.

Death nurturing life.

My heart is heavy as a piece of it is buried
Among all those papers, memories,
friends, fantasies and dreams.

The seeds of hope for new life are also buried
Among these discarded pieces.

New beginnings, nourishment and joy will germinate.

New Year's Eve was celebrated by our entire family at Loma Linda. And Grandma Gyori was brought over to celebrate the completion of our new home. This house had been transformed into a beautiful, restful, functional living space. We had all the creature comforts we could wish for. It was a joy to work in the kitchen. The study promised to become an inviting room for creative responses to critical issues of our time. We could now relax in our living room before a dancing fire. It was fitting that Tom and I could end 1998 alone, together, quietly reveling in God's blessings and provisions. Thanks be to God!

We Say Goodbye to Grandma Gyori

> *Down in the dust I lie;*
>   *Give me life according to your word.*
> *I was honest about my past way, and you answered me;*
>   *Teach me your statutes.*
> *Make me understand the way of your precepts,*
>   *And I will meditate on your wondrous deeds.*
> *My soul is weary with sorrow;*
>   *Strengthen me according to your word.*
>   **PSALM 119:25,28**

Elizabeth Stromayer Gyori was born in Budapest, Hungary, and immigrated to the United States as a child. Her family settled in Chicago, where she lived most of her life. Lamentably, after graduating from high school, she did not pursue further education. I always felt she could have become an accomplished, professional businesswoman. She met her future husband Julius, at a Hungarian dance and they subsequently married and moved into an apartment on the north side of Chicago.

Tom was their only child, and they provided him with loving care. Julius had rejected Christianity early in his life, and Elizabeth became a devotee of a Hindu teacher. They didn't understand Tom's "conversion" experience and seemed a bit disconcerted by his decision to go to seminary, but they wisely supported his career choice. I felt very welcome into their family and enjoyed their warm hospitality over the years.

In 1980, we accepted Grandma Gyori's offer to make our home in the second floor apartment of her residence. We lived there for the next twenty years. During her waning years, it became increasingly challenging for me to care for her as compassionately as I would have liked. I attributed my discontent to the differences that existed between us. In hindsight, it seems I have much to learn about people whose views and life experiences differ from my own. I quote a Guatemalan Pentecostal theologian, Nestor Medina, who recently wrote, "Diverse peoples are celebrated as heirs to diverse forms of knowledge and life experiences." I need to celebrate her "diverse forms of knowledge and life experiences."

Our entire family knew her as a genuinely kind and profoundly generous woman. Her wisdom and knowledge of the city of Chicago was appreciated by each of us. She was deeply loved and respected by her grandchildren in whom she took great pride. All have been impacted by her loyalty to the Chicago Cubs. To this day the Gyoris are all enthusiastic Cubs fans. To become a member of the Gyori clan, one had to be taught how to play pinochle by Grandma Gyori! We lovingly shared many of her tasty recipes at her funeral service which was presided over by Tom on February 20, 1999, at the Ravenswood Presbyterian Church.

CHAPTER 23

Peaceweavings

See how good, how pleasant it is
For God's people to live together as one!
PSALM 133:1

G od was planting seeds which were germinating below the surface. One of those was building an intentional community which gradually became defined for both Tom and me. In the fall of 1994, Ross Kinsler sent us his manuscript of *The Biblical Jubilee and the Struggle for Life*. He and his wife Gloria had written this book together and asked us to review it prior to publication. A small group of us had been discussing community living and decided to read the Kinsler's book together. Researching community living in the light of the biblical Jubilee became all-consuming for this nucleus of believers. We read of other groups experimenting with this idea as well as visiting some well-established Christian intentional communities which helped us define what might be entailed in such a venture.

Lee Van Ham responded to my invitation to share from his own experience of this experiment. He was one of the original members of "Peaceweavings", the name of our intentional community. Here is his response:

> "Peaceweavings continually brought joy and challenges to me. My consciousness on some relationships and issues lagged. I needed the transformation that an intentional community can prod. I'm deeply grateful for the experience and for the day when the Gyoris made a great living space possible.
>
> "Grace and Tom came to one of our potluck gatherings with a possibility that made the vision possible. Ever so hesitantly, they said, 'It may not fit at all, but because Tom's mother has recently passed, the property we have on St. Louis Street is available. Having an intentional community there would fit our dream.'"

To bring this dream to fruition, we worked together to rehabilitate the two flats at 3913 N. St. Louis, which had been the Gyori residence for so many years. This entailed eliminating the second-floor kitchen, turning that space into another living area for a resident. Likewise, we adapted the basement into space where Tom and I stayed. We learned how to share one kitchen and the multiple household tasks during endless meetings and to amicably share the differently designated living spaces. More significant to learning to live together was the opportunity to share our lives on deeper levels and with the broader activist community in Chicago. Every Thursday we hosted a potluck dinner attended by a wide variety of guests; this engendered thought-provoking discussions of issues of relevance to us all. Tasks and expenses were all shared.

At least twenty-five individuals made this community their home for varying periods of time. Among these were two different families who had to leave Colombia, their home country, for their safety. Lives were deeply impacted as we shared not only living space, but so much of ourselves and our experiences, initiating life-long friendships holding fast to this day.

My expectations of Peaceweavings becoming a shared property, with long-term commitments by its members, proved unrealistic. Instead, we were able to provide a welcoming, safe home to individuals and families needing temporary housing over the span of ten years. In the end, Tom and I never lived full time in that community because we had made the decision to rehabilitate Loma Linda into our lovely primary residence, spending most weekends at "3913", in Chicago. There is little doubt that each member of Peaceweavings left feeling their life had been enriched by living together. Now we are scattered from Colombia to California, and Chicago to central Indiana.

Son Jim bought the building after we dismantled Peaceweavings. He has now refurbished it and returned the building to its original two apartments, which he is successfully renting out. And so, "3913" remains in the Gyori family's possession and provides comfortable housing to new residents.

Western Adventures

The Peaceweavings community was happily establishing itself in Chicago and our first spring in our own home in Loma Linda was delightful. We decided to embark on a full-fledged celebration of retirement by fulfilling the dream of exploring the West. Vivi, Jim and Niko joined us. This was Vivi's introduction to camping which was impacted by her being several months pregnant. We were finishing packing up camping gear and other necessities into our VW camper when Niko stepped out of the open door without realizing how far it was off the sidewalk. He fell face-down on the cement cutting his lip, painfully interrupting his excitement for the trip. Without further delay, we left Chicago in two vehicles, Jim and family in our green Ambassador, and Tom and I in the VW.

We camped at nights along the way and enjoyed swimming pools when available until we arrived in the Black Hills. There we enjoyed a visit to Mt. Rushmore and the Crazy Horse Monument. We were exposed to fascinating landscapes found only in that region. On day six, we arrived at Yellowstone National Park. We enjoyed the wonders of this magnificent park complete with fishing, seeing bison and other animals and, of course, the spectacular geysers. What a trooper Vivi was! Fishing every day was something she enjoyed, but she was not enamored with sleeping in a tent every night especially when temperatures plunged below freezing. She was ready to turn around and go home. As planned, we separated, and they made their way back to Chicago while Tom and I stayed a few days longer for more exploring, including a delightful trip to the nearby Grand Tetons. We exulted in the grandeur of God's creation and our unmerited privilege to be able to travel into this wonderland of breath-taking vistas. Words fail.

A weekend visit in Spokane, Washington, included memorable time with Jim and Genette Emery. It was clear that Jim's health was declining, but he engaged us in his usual cryptic conversations. On August 3, we arrived in Edmonds, Washington, for a visit with Ken, Bea, and Paul, in their lovely home. During the ten days we stayed with them, we enjoyed time on their boat on Lake Washington, watching the grand display of the Blue Angels performing in their six jet planes. While we were with them, they had to choose which child they would adopt from an orphanage in the Ukraine. This was very difficult, but in the end, they have never regretted their choice of Tatiana. Now began their preparations for including her in their family.

Tom and I had made reservations for a week's stay at Holden Village on the eastern side of the Cascade Mountains. Here's how I tried to capture this experience in words:

Too much beauty surrounds me;
Towering, craggy peaks
With snow outlining crevices,
Rushing mountain streams,
Singing around each twist and turn.

Stately pines dominate the green forest,
God's pristine creation, full of LIFE.

Fascinating people, old and young.

Some seeking new direction,
Others missing microwaves.

Teaching staff with varied offerings
Comprise this retreat center.

Good conversations with new friends.

Challenging long hikes
Followed by renewing soaks in a jacuzzi.

We've enjoyed the gift of tranquility,
Breathtaking vistas of emerald Heart Lake,
Fed by a towering waterfall.

Reluctantly, we return to "normality"
And new adventures await us.

We left the grandeurs of Washington State and drove south down Oregon's and California's coastal highway. I called Gloria Kinsler during a stop in Portland to plan for visiting them in Altadena, California. She shared the sad news that Jim Emery had just died that day. We decided to continue our journey until we reached San Jose, California, where we would board a plane for Spokane, where Tom had been invited to participate in Jim's funeral. In Spokane, Kateri, a friend from Chicago, met our plane and hosted us in her home during our time there. We were reunited with Ralph Winter, a former colleague from Guatemala, who also participated in the memorial service for Jim. We enjoyed meeting the Emery family and were assured by their support of Gennett in the grieving of their loss.

Returning to Santa Cruz by air, we were on the road again. We drove to Los Angeles where we were delighted to stay with Rachel Lausch and David Winters. A joy-filled visit with Gloria and Ross Kinsler in nearby Altadena introduced us to their son Paul's wife, Michelle. We took advantage of being near Westminster Gardens, a Presbyterian retirement home. There we greeted more Guatemalan colleagues, Bob and Bernice Thorp, Dick Wallis and Vera Ainley. After another night with the Kinslers, we left at 3 a.m. for the next leg of our journey, across the desert and all the way to Albuquerque, New Mexico. Here we were warmly welcomed by Hilda and Don

Wales and Ruth and John Hazelton. How we enjoyed lively conversations filled with laughter and shared memories.

'Dreamcatcher' was the name we had given our VW Vanagon, home-away-from-home. She had been complaining a bit until this mega stretch. Now she demanded more than a mere push to start her engine. Don and Tom took her in for repairs. Honoring her growing uncertainty, we decided to drive home via the shortest, least interesting route. We made our way through Texas, Oklahoma, Missouri, and Illinois. After exciting adventures and glorious reunions with so many friends, we were glad to return home to Loma Linda.

CHAPTER 24

Focus on Family

Children are the heritage God gives us;
Our descendants are our rewards.

PSALM 127

May you live to see your children's children.

PSALM 128:6

We felt like we needed a vacation from our vacation after returning to Loma Linda. Reconnecting with our children became our priority. In mid-September 1999, we drove to Raleigh to stay with Tom and Lisa's four children while their parents made their well-deserved trip to New Zealand. We were greeted by news of hurricane Floyd making its way up the eastern coast from the Bahamas. Fortunately, we were not affected by its fury. How we enjoyed our time, cementing loving relationships with these fascinating four grandchildren, Sarah, Chris, Austin and Nathan!

In October, we went to Elkhart to make applesauce with Sonja and spend a couple of days playing with Erin and James

On October 24, Isabella Marie was born to Vivi and Jim. Vivi's mom had flown to Chicago, to be with them and was so helpful as their family welcomed their second child.

> *Music plays in the background,*
> *Flames dance in the fireplace.*
>
> *Gusty winds blow tenacious gold,*
> *red and green leaves.*
>
> *The sun makes the leaves sparkle*
> *Like gems against black clouds.*
>
> *My pulse quickens with anticipation and anxiety,*
> *A bit restless like the leaves.*
>
> *What tasks need completion this week,*
> *Before leaving for Edmonds?*

Ken and Bea were informed they were to be in Ukraine to pick up their new baby, Tatiana Marie, by Bea Oct. 30. This meant Tom and I were soon on our way to their home in Edmonds, Washington, to stay with Paul during their absence. We were instructed in the rhythms of their life and thoroughly enjoyed building our respect and care for Paul.

While there, I was nurtured by Thomas Moore's book, *Care of the Soul.* "Family with its joys and pains forms the crucible of every individual's soul," is a quote which resonated with me. Tatiana was plucked from a good Ukrainian orphanage by two strangers. She was whisked away by train, bus, and plane to begin a new life across the globe by two adoring parents who gave her more love and attention than she had experienced during her eight months of life. Big brother Paul welcomed her with loving excitement, matched by our own. Tom was honored to officiate at her baptism days before a celebrative Thanksgiving.

1999 ended with joyful fanfare, as we enjoyed a gathering of most of our extended family in and around Chicago, including sister Rosaline and daughter Catherine from Windsor, Ontario.

We bade farewell to a century and enjoyed the extravagant fireworks around the globe, via television, welcoming in the year 2000. Once in a lifetime spectacle, indeed!

Loma Linda, Our New Home

> *May God give you your heart's desires*
> *And fulfill all your dreams!*
>
> **PSALM 20:4**

Loma Linda provided us a new home for the new year and century. What a sense of accomplishment and contentment we enjoyed as we sat before the crackling fire, sipping coffee, alone together, thoroughly enjoying our new life of retirement. So many dreams were fulfilled. We now had the time and opportunity to process the innumerable life experiences we had shared and now anticipated new ones. We looked forward to sharing our lovely home with family and friends, which indeed became a regular part of our lives in Beverly Shores, Indiana, where Loma Linda resided. I was particularly refreshed, sitting on our front deck and watching the seasons change as winter morphed into spring. I was enamored with the arrival of innumerable birds on their flight paths north. It was exciting to learn from sister Rosaline how to identify these lovely creatures. Watching trees and shrubs explode into myriad shades of green and lovely blossoms made me rejoice anew in God's evolving creation.

We both enjoyed offering hospitality. Our church family at Lake View Presbyterian Church in Chicago ritually blessed our house, as they moved from room to room asking God's blessings. A dinner honoring all who had worked on the reconstruction was a joy to share. Soon we welcomed friends from Cuba, Brazil, and Ecuador, along with family from Washington to North Carolina.

Our home was located about a mile from the South Shore train. This allowed me independence and easy access to activities and responsibilities in Chicago. We regularly spent weekends in the city, participating in activities, both at Peaceweavings and at Lake View Church.

Our individual travels continued, with Tom going to Cuba again. One memorable moment came when Tom called to say he had left his passport at home. He waited in Nassau for me to send it. After untoward delays, it arrived, and he joined his delegation in Havana.

In mid-January, I was honored to lead a group of ecumenical religious leaders from the Americas, sponsored by SIPAZ, on a delegation to Chiapas in southern Mexico. Rev. John Sinclair, our former "boss" while we served in Guatemala, was a member of this group. In the town of Tzajalchen, our first stop out of San Cristobal, we received a warm reception by the local Catholic Church. A three-hour mass, outside in the blazing sun, proved to be a heart-warming inspiration! I was drawn to their prayers of the people described reverently as "inverted rain showers of petitions rising to water the heart of God."

Back in San Cristobal, Bishop Samuel Ruiz welcomed us enthusiastically. We participated in several celebrations of his forty years of service in Chiapas. A grand finale, filled with pomp and circumstance, was held in the plaza before the cathedral.

What a treat to return to lovely, quiet, Loma Linda after exhausting travels! Journaling allowed me to capture these extraordinary experiences and record them into the marvelous gift box of memory. Nevertheless, here's a piece I wrote soon after returning from Mexico:

"My life speeds along at breakneck speed. It interfaces with rich and diverse relationships, friends, family, and communities. Just when I anticipate a space of time to withdraw into a 'sabbath', a plethora of demands descend on me. Correspondence, reports, gardening, laundry, sewing, preparations for upcoming travels, maintaining relationships with Peaceweavings—all require attention." Fortunately, reflective sabbath moments helped meet "my heart's desires."

Juanita and Lee Mangan-Van Ham joined us in a memorable trip to Ghost Ranch, near Abiquiu, New Mexico. We traveled together in our VW Vanagon, "Dreamcatcher." At the Ranch, we enjoyed lectures presented by Gloria and Ross Kinsler who developed the theme of Jubilee with insightful clarity. We were proud to claim them as close friends. Anna and Don Sibley, former colleagues in Guatemala, were also participants. Together we were all challenged by the biblical imperative of living justice for all of God's creation as it was detailed in the biblical call to an alternative way of living. While there, we again connected with Ruth and John Hazelton, and Hilda and Don Wales, who lived nearby. Years before, John Sinclair had told us, "Your most long-lasting friendships will be your missionary colleagues." That certainly has been our experience after fifty years of knowing each other.

CHAPTER 25

Jubilee Economics Ministries (JEM)

We received the generous gift of the seeds of JEM from Gloria and Ross Kinsler. The seeds were imbedded in the manuscript of their book, The *Biblical Jubilee and the Struggle for Life*, published in 1999 by Orbis Books. Upon returning to Chicago from Ghost Ranch, we joined with others in carefully planting these seeds in the fertile ground of Peaceweavings, where they began to sprout into healthy seedlings. A board of directors ensued, and the cultivation of the young plants developed. Lee articulated two core questions related to Jubilee Economics:

- What does an economy look like that requires the resources of only one planet?
- How do we practice it?

Ched Myers summarized three axioms in his "Foreword" to *The Biblical Jubilee and the Struggle for Life*:

- "The world as created by God is abundant, with enough for everyone—provided that human communities restrain their appetites and live within limits.

- Disparities in wealth are not "natural" but the result of human sin and must be mitigated within the community of faith through the regular practice of wealth distribution.
- The prophetic message calls people to the practice of such redistribution and is thus characterized as "good news" to the poor. (A good definition of Jubilee.)"

In 2002, a core group in Chicago, all of whom were devoted to Jubilee practices, was hit by a transplant of Jubilee seedlings that sent participants in several directions. Lee carefully transported some in San Diego, California, when he and Juanita moved there. The plants now forming began to adopt a life of their own. Because JEM's understanding of Jubilee was not widely understood, Jubilee took on the adjective One Earth and became One Earth Jubilee, readily conveying the commitment to living within our planet's resources in contrast to the MultiEarth ways of the American Dream.

Another important "gardener" tending these shoots was Dan Swanson, an active member of a Mexican/American congregation in the La Villita neighborhood of Chicago. Dan worked closely with Peaceweavings and was a partner in launching JEM. For Dan's part, after marrying Dr. Angelica Juarez, they built a home on Angelica's family plot in the village of San Mateo, outside Puebla, Mexico, and took up residence there. From there they transplanted JEM seedlings into productive soil in both San Mateo and in San Cristobal in Mexico's southern state of Chiapas. By 2015, JEM had become bi-national with Dan, directing in Mexico and Lee in San Diego.

When Dan suddenly died in December 2016, the Cultural Center in San Mateo, a busy garden of Jubilee ministries, became the Daniel Swanson Cultural Center. In the wake of Dan's death, Angelica and the people they'd touched with Jubilee continued cultivating the garden, creatively. A Jubilee Circle of participants formed in both San Mateo and San Cristobal. Learning from them, San Diego also began forming a Jubilee Circle. The flourishing, fruitful saplings of Jubilee Economics Ministries prosper now with international flavors under competent, nurturing gardeners.

Upheavals

SEPTEMBER 11, 2001
You (the Lord) trace my journeying
   And my resting places,
   And are familiar with all the paths I take.
PSALM 139:3

Loma Linda had become our beloved "resting place" during this first year of a new century, and the first full year of living in our lovely, new home. We exercised our gifts of hospitality with joy. So many fun-filled days spent with our extended family from near and far. After time playing on the beach, we frequently enjoyed eating delicious barbecued meals. Friends stopped by for differing lengths of time. There were enriching conversations and shared experiences which covered the spectrum of theology and politics. Tom and I were renewed in reading books and expanding our mutual understandings of Jubilee, feminism and ecology. My times of private reflection and journaling deepened my faith. In many ways, this was the beginning of the happiest years of our married life. I wrote often of sitting on the deck with coffee in hand, watching the evolving phases of seasons, flora and fauna, and the antics of our dog, Sparky, playing with deer, squirrels, and other critters who happened by. Birdsong filled the air, and identifying new birds became a hobby on cooler days, hours before the indoor fire elicited profound gratitude. Rest and solitude between entertaining became our new norm, until we hit the road again.

Tom had been invited to perform his cousin Karl and Cresencia's wedding on Sunday, September 16, in Washington, D.C. On our way there we drove through Raleigh for a delightful visit with Tom Jr. and his family. Friends of theirs loaned us the use of their cabin for a few days. It was on Holden Beach, on the Atlantic coast of North Carolina. What a treat to be sleeping across the street from the Atlantic Ocean! On Tuesday morning, September 11, I was seated at the beach, eating an apple, watching a surfer, and journaling, when Tom came running from the house exclaiming that the World Trade Towers in New York City had been attacked by passenger planes flown directly into the buildings around nine a.m. My first thoughts were, "The U.S. is no longer invulnerable. We are reaping the fruits of our dominance and intransigence!" All U.S. aircraft were immediately grounded. Who knew what other actions the Bush administration would call for?

Tom and I watched the developing news on television. Across the nation, people gathered in houses of worship to pray during this frightening time. Network news was filled with reports of first responders and survivors, as well as the mounting number of fatalities. The administration's first inclinations seemed to focus on naming culprits and promising revenge. How does one pray under such dire circumstances?

News of a similar attack on the Pentagon and a third in Pennsylvania only added to the horror. Together, Tom and I had yet a couple of days to process all of this before returning briefly to Raleigh. I was surprised when Chris informed us that the students in his school were prohibited from even talking about these attacks.

We went to Washington on Friday and drove past the still-smoking Pentagon which had also been struck by a plane. We met with many of the Stromayer family who were gathering to celebrate the planned wedding. Karl's brother Eric was their best man, but he and his wife Susmita were stationed in a U.S. embassy out of the country. We all awaited with bated breath to learn if they would be able to find a flight to D.C. They arrived safely about 10 p.m. Saturday evening. The ceremony took place on the banks of the Potomac River, in a lovely park. Tom did a superb job of weaving together the tragedy with spirituality and their marriage commitment to each other. It was a thoroughly happy occasion, all but overshadowed by calamity. Joyfully celebrating with extended family proved to be a rich antidote to all that was occurring around us.

Back in Chicago, the upheaval caused by 9/11 was felt all around us, specifically in Peaceweavings and in Lake View Church. Sundays proved to be the most engaging days during the rest of September. At church, we took part in the leadership of discussions centered around people's search for faithful responses. During this time, I journaled: "I'm feeling overwhelmed by the enormity of the implications of war and the apparent apathy of some church leaders not knowing how to respond. Protest marches, written pronouncements, even prayer vigils feel so inadequate. Some people would focus on our great nation and the preserving of our freedoms, others on protecting ourselves from future attacks. Still others on exploring/understanding why we were attacked in the first place. How can we all move beyond personal ego needs and be open to listen to each other without condemnation and somehow forge a more unified, Spirit-led, faithful response?" All of life seemed so disrupted.

Later, as I reflected on the ambiguities of the frequently named War on Terror, I wrote: "This is no conventional war. There is no nation state against whom to declare war. No one with whom to negotiate a settlement, no international laws to argue, no armies to pit against each other. In my opinion, no war can be justified. How will winners and losers be determined? When, by whom? This war seems to be waged in secret. No press is allowed to cover Afghan civilian casualties. Our administration pre-empted humanitarian concerns early on, by very publicly dropping a few bundles of 'aid' for fleeing refugees in the midst of active mine fields. What new high-tech weapons are we testing? My guess is: war machines that can operate effectively in harsh, cold, mountainous environments, too often without any human pilot to witness the dying. Pinpoint accuracy, indeed!"

"The reporting of this war is endless affirmation of our country's domestic and international support for endless sorties and successful launching of 'smart' and 'seismic' bombs. Little mention is made of ongoing protest actions, inter-religious calls for cessation of attacks, or publication of the impressive stream of scholarly, 'faith-full' judgments from around the world. We, in the resistance, are meant to feel immobilized, powerless and ultimately ineffective."

Juanita concluded that the physical ambience of Chicago was too toxic for her asthmatic condition. She felt compelled to find a healthier environment in which to live. After extended research, San Diego became Juanita and Lee's choice of a new home. Several of Juanita's family already had moved there, which made the choice most compelling. Could Peaceweavings withstand such a departure? In many ways, this couple seemed the veritable glue holding the community together. Thoughtful discernment was carefully done by one and all to envision and plan for their departure.

Before Juanita and Lee departed for their new life, we had lengthy conversations about the future of Peaceweavings. We discussed the possibility of defining ourselves as a Sabbath Jubilee community. What might that entail? Some suggestions were: agree on a common day to honor the Sabbath, agree on a biblical text to focus the day, celebrate a specific ritual, pray, fast and break the fast with a common meal in the evening. We agreed to call a community meeting on Jan. 21 to begin fleshing out these ideas concretely.

The dreaded day arrived when we tearfully bade Juanita and Lee farewell as they departed in a jam-packed rented truck holding all their earthly belongings. I wrote, "Peaceweavings feels empty, our hearts mourn. Do we have enough love and forgiveness to carry on and move forward?". Our beloved leaders had left.

War Resistance

> *I have lived too long with belligerent people!*
> *I stand for peace,*
>   *But when I talk of peace, they want war!*
>   **PSALM 120:6,7**

A growing number of organizations were forming in attempts to resist our nation's propensity for responding to conflicts around the world with armed force, too often utilizing our own military as in the "war on terror." Because of our connections with Latin America, the peacemaking groups we related to focused on U.S. interventions in that region.

Ft. Benning, Georgia, was the home of the School of Americas, where military men from Central American were trained in military tactics to subvert the "threat of communism" perceived in the region. The School of Americas Watch (SOA Watch) is a prime example of a well-organized protest movement. In 1983, Father Roy Bourgeois, a Jesuit priest, climbed a tree on the Ft. Benning military base in Columbus, Georgia, and took a loud speaker up with him. There he played a recording of Archbishop Oscar Romero's sermon calling on the Salvadoran military to stop killing their own people and lay down their arms in obedience to God. He was jailed for 18 months for that action. In 1990, on the first anniversary of the massacre of Jesuit priests in San Salvador, Father Roy was joined by a few other people in a water only fast. This action was the seed that grew into a nation-wide movement. Every November until 2015, hundreds of people gathered at the gates of Ft. Benning to protest the training of Latin American military personnel in military tactics. These were festive occasions, complete with street theatre, inspiring music, rousing speeches and testimonials from Central Americans directly affected by military actions in their countries. Tom and I went to Ft. Benning at least twice and were re-energized by these nonviolent actions. Many arrests were made of people who climbed or penetrated the imposing fencing constructed around the entrance to the base. SOA Watch provided legal counseling for those who had decided to breach the fence, and support groups formed for them, as well.

Witness for Peace and SIPAZ were among a plethora of organizations committed to nonviolent peacemaking. These two I have written about and of my participation in them. Another group which I supported though not with my participation was Christian Peacemaking Teams (CPT). It was formed soon after Witness for Peace. Gene Stoltzfus, its founder, traveled with me on the first WFP delegation. Members of CPT primarily come from the "peace churches" such as the Mennonite Church and the Church of the Brethren. CPT continues to this day, sending volunteers into places of conflict. These accompaniers of people are trained in how to witness nonviolently in hotspots. They accompany people threatened in Israel/Palestine, Iraqi Kurdistan, Colombia, the U.S./Mexico border, and to some eastern Canadian tribal lands. Peace Brigades International is another accompaniment program, calling on volunteers from many nations to participate. The Presbyterian Peace Fellowship sponsors an accompaniment program in Colombia and on our border with Mexico, as well. Together, these groups, many motivated by their faith, are able to raise the awareness of people in our country, with the hope of influencing political power brokers to confront the military/industrial complex which continues to profit from arms sales and warmongering

The challenge I felt was how to articulate convincingly the import of our years of learning and experiencing about conflicts and nonviolent responses. In church settings, I felt hesitant to impose yet another issue upon full agendas, such as how to nurture peacemaking in Central America or Israel/Palestine. Folks at Lake View Presbyterian Church were already advocating for gay rights, confronting inner-city violence in Chicago and Aids prevention/cure. They were also fundraising for their building restoration project. Both Tom and I were given numerous opportunities to share our concerns with the congregation, but often I felt very inadequate in my ability to lead people to creative responses to our presentations.

We dedicated much time and energy in trying to understand and model our learnings about the biblical Jubilee. The Peaceweavings Community should have been the ideal setting for "living out" these important themes. I anguished over the difficulty of explaining Jubilee to family and friends. These conflictive feelings occurred simultaneously with President Bush's persistent push to invade Iraq. This enraged me! Yet another example of our nation's bent toward warmongering. History now clearly shows how ill advised that initiative was. That conflict propelled our country into a never-ending war in the Middle East.

In 2019 I was escorted to the 30th anniversary of the founding of the Chicago Religious Leadership Network on Latin America, CRLN, by Gary Cozette. Gary became both friend and mentor in the 1980's when we worked together in

Chicago. With the sponsorship of the Presbytery of Chicago, Gary went to El Salvador during the conflicts there. Gary documented human rights violations, communicated them to us in Chicago and we in turn advised people via an extended phone tree across the U.S., who then informed both elected officials and local churches of the atrocities. I am most grateful to Gary for becoming my first gay friend, introducing me to a new appreciation of gender identities different from my own. My life has been profoundly impacted by my many LGBTQ friends ever since for which I praise God.

CHAPTER 26

Re-Examining Faith and Life

O God, from my youth you have taught me,
  And I still proclaim your wondrous deeds.
So even to old age and grey hairs,
  O God, do not forsake me,
  until I proclaim your might
  to all the generations to come.
Your power and your righteousness, O God,
  reach the high heavens.

PSALM 71:17–19

I felt the need to share the reasons for our advocacy work, for our commitment to justice, nonviolence, peacemaking, community living, and earthkeeping. The bottom line is we believe God has extended justice, compassion and generosity to us, therefore expects no less of us.

On February 20, 2003 I wrote:

Too fast. Slow down!

The train's speed catches my breath.

I must choose to apply the brakes, or disembark.

Back and forth, in and out,
Chicago, here we come.

Meeting, child care, meeting.

Birthday party, meeting.

Emotional, physical stress.

Celebration, chaos, fun.

Conversations, strategizing.

Even naps tucked in.

Too much, too fast: SLOW DOWN!

Although Juanita and Lee had moved to San Diego, leaving Peaceweavings bereft of their expanding vision and skilled leadership, we maintained regular communication with them. Juanita continued to share her creative gifts and wisdom with me.

These two years of 2003–4 were challenging for Tom and me because of the ongoing "busyness" of our lives. Our shared vision of Peaceweavings becoming a Jubilee House never materialized into the reality we had hoped for, despite our developing a document to help guide us. Instead, Peaceweavings seemed to develop organically with the passage of time, as members transitioned. As a community, we agreed to welcome a Colombian family who needed housing after leaving their home country due to threats upon their lives. Constanza Valencia and her two children, Santiago and Adriana, lived with us for several years before moving into an independent apartment. Later, another couple from Colombia joined us for a shorter time. Sharing life with such a disparate group of people kept us all on our toes, as we negotiated fulfillment of agreed-upon tasks, moving into different living spaces, and

Tom and I being present only on weekends. The joys far out-
weighed the discomforts of this experiment in communal living. We all were enriched and empowered by the visitors who
shared meals and new learnings with us regularly.

Our various commitments at Lake View Church demanded
much time as well. Tom's involvements included work with
Chicago Presbytery and my ongoing work was with the Chicago Sanctuary Movement and the Chicago Religious Leadership Network on Latin America, I also accepted opportunities
to translate for Spanish speakers.

Sophia/Wisdom

I long for you, search for you, desperately need you.

Reveal yourself to me in epiphany,
In 'showings and encounters'.

Wisdom is bright, and does not grow dim.

By those who love her she is readily seen
and found by those who look for her.

She makes herself known to them.

Watch for her early and you will have no trouble;
You will find her sitting at your gates.

— Jan Richardson

Mentors and Friends

We met in Guatemala City in the early 1970's. Little did I know
what a transforming impact Guatemalan poet/theologian Julia Esquivel would have on my entire being! Let's start with
this irresistible challenge she articulated in 1988, written in
Managua, Nicaragua.

ON THE MARCH!

Titanic task,
a divine task, ours:
to make ourselves human!

On the march!

Knocking down idols
breaking chains
tearing free!

On the march!

Relinquishing ourselves,
advancing, stumbling, falling,
and rising again!

Moving on!

Fix your eyes always on utopia,
on that lost paradise
always present and always distant.

Powerful magnet,
unrecognized strength, denied, attacked
by anti-humans.

Vocation, first
and final,
a thousand times lost
a thousand times found.

Sole possibility
to live with meaning
to know life
to fuse with her intimately,
illuminated!

— from *The Certainty of Spring,*
Poems by a Guatemalan in Exile

When we first met, Julia had recently left her seminary studies in San Jose, Costa Rica, recognizing that the Presbyterian Church of Guatemala did not ordain women, and she needed to care for her mother. Back home in Guatemala she worked with incarcerated youth and street children in the capital city. Her insights into the causes of the poverty of these kids were revelatory to me. Being an accomplished journalist, she began publishing a provocative paper, "Dialogo", denouncing by name some people in high places whom she held responsible for human rights abuses in the country. It was not long before she was exiled and fled to Switzerland. There she lived in the ecumenical monastic community of Granchamp from 1980 to 1987. We corresponded during that time, and little did I know she was writing some of her to-be-published poetry, for which she has become recognized as a gifted poet and theologian. Years passed, Guatemala descended into brutal violence toward its majority indigenous population, and was ruled by a ruthless "Christian" dictator, Efrain Rios Montt. A modicum of justice has been made by his being found guilty of high crimes and misdemeanors and today is incarcerated. In 2015, I spent a delightful, sacred afternoon with Julia in her home in Guatemala City, sharing fond memories. An unforgettable mentor indeed!

As I wrote earlier, during our missionary orientation, we had been told to expect that our missionary colleagues would become our most enduring, life-long friends. For Tom and me that has born rich fruit. To this day, my regular phone conversations with Ross and Gloria Kinsler, partners in Guatemala, Ruth Hazelton, Mexico, Hilda and Don Wales, Chile and Mexico, Rachel Lausch, Guatemala, and Barbara Frost, Guatemala, and frequent correspondence from Karla Koll, Costa Rica, and Dennis and Maribel Smith, Argentina, nourish and inform me as dear, dear friends.

One of these was Linda Jones. She and her husband Dave had served as Presbyterian short term missionaries in Korea during the lethal, political uprisings in that country in the 1970's and '80's. Linda's and my paths crossed frequently in our human rights advocacy work within Presbyterian circles, she with a razor-sharp focus on Korea, and I with my experiences in Central America. After working as a public-school teacher for years, Linda had felt the call to ordained ministry and had enrolled in McCormick Theological Seminary, a Presbyterian school in Chicago. She did her Clinical Practical Education in the federal prison in Michigan City. She lived with us at Loma Linda during those three months of training.

Linda was diagnosed with leukemia during that time, and I felt called to spend time with her every Monday afternoon, in her home in Des Plaines, Illinois, after she left our home. Those hours became rich times of learning and reflection for both of us. She taught me so much about faithful witness to gospel truths and brave responses to political injustices as she had lived them in Korea. She was part of the editorial group which wrote the book *More Than Witnesses*, detailing the amazing stories of activities of the "Monday Night Group" of missionaries in Korea who acted as liaisons for young Koreans who were fighting against the brutal authoritarian government in power. Linda had carefully documented the activities of that period and had stored innumerable documents in her basement.

After the overthrow of the harsh regime, and the installation of the new democratic government, she decided that those papers belonged in Korea, not Des Plaines. Together, we boxed them up. Several of the "Monday Night Group" were officially invited to accompany these documents back to Korea. They were welcomed with pomp and ceremony by the president and other officials. How exciting it was for me to learn of all of this during my Monday visits with Linda. Linda finally succumbed to her fatal illness, and I mourn her absence. This inspirational friendship deepened and led me to write this poem, extolling the yiddish word "dayenu."

Dayenu!

Gratitude for my soul-sisters, Juanita and Linda

Had God only brought us together to share
Our growing passion for justice and peace
And not let us see those dreams fulfilled, Dayenu!

(That would be enough!)

Had God not cared for us together
During times of spiritual and physical brokenness
And not ordained us to optimal health, Dayenu!

(That would be enough!)

Had God not gifted us with "bird-marveling"
And inspiring "deck-time" at Loma Linda
And not blessed us with more hallowed times together, Dayenu!

(That would be enough!)

Had God not provided us opportunities
To share our soul journeys, moving us out of our comfort zones,
And did not let us continue traveling together, Dayenu!

(That would be enough!)

Our involvement with expanding family provided much joy. We never tired of welcoming them into our home. The celebration of my 70th birthday was a beautiful example of these exciting events. I was genuinely surprised to see Naomi and David Helmuth, Ray's parents, as well as Laura Fusco, Bea's mom, along with our four children and their offspring. The crowning gift was a new diamond ring which Tom ceremoniously gave me. What fun it was to receive a gift from each person. There was Nathan's drawing of him with me on Mt. Baldy. Erin gave me a waffle/pancake mix. Tatiana gave me a pinecone, remembering how she and I gathered pine cones together for our fire place. Each gift was later acknowledged by hand-decorated thank you notes from me.

This event added to our annual Christmas celebrations in different church fellowship halls, over the years. These spaces allowed us the room we needed to both share Christmas tamales as well as areas for sharing Christmas reflections and play. What glorious memories remain of these times spent enjoying each other.

CHAPTER 27

Leaving Loma Linda

I could fly away with wings made of dawn,
Or make my home on the far side of the sea,
But even there your hand will guide me.
PSALM 139:9, 10

Plainfield, Indiana, was hardly the "far side of the sea," but that was our destination. Sonja and Ray had invited us to live with them when we decided we could no longer manage life at Loma Linda on our own. We felt God guiding us to make the move in 2011. We were well aware of the daunting tasks ahead of us; downsizing yet again, preparing the house for sale, finding the right buyer, packing and finally taking our leave. All these activities were completed with dispatch and hard work. We were so grateful for help from many family members and friends, including Jim's decisiveness in disposing of unneeded items after consulting with us, of course. This tranquil property was the only one we ever owned and lived on as our primary residence. Happy memories will always linger as we recall the joys of hosting so many friends and relatives over the previous twelve years.

Ray had accepted the invitation to become the principal of the Van Buren Elementary School in Plainfield, Indiana, a couple of years before. They were completing an addition to their home in which to accommodate us. Upon finishing that renovation, we sadly left our beloved Loma Linda, to begin a new life just west of Indianapolis.

A New Life Opens in Plainfield

Our God guards our leaving and our coming back,
  Now and forever.
                                                    PSALM 121:8

To accommodate us, Sonja and Ray made many adjustments to their lives. A major one was to build a new master bedroom suite onto their existing house, for themselves. They designated for us the original and renovated master bedroom with an adjacent deck. During the 2020 COVID pandemic, I described the view which welcomed us every day.

Spring from my Window

"I open the blinds and see a microcosm of God's magnificent creation displayed, invoking celebration in quarantine!

  "Breathtaking beauty engages all of my senses as I look out of my window. Water tumbling gently over rocks, falls into the pond in front and center. Water lilies and water irises promise brilliant blooms next month. Among the rocks rest seashells, proudly displaying their unique shapes crafted by unknown seas. The greening lilac bush dominates the far side of the pond, its fragrant buds almost ready to *explode their distinct aromas. Hovering over the lilac is a stunning redbud tree in full bloom.*

"Some empty pots await the brilliant faces of gerbera daisies and dahlias to be planted. The stalwart blue-bottle tree reigns in the corner over a collection of colored rocks which will be placed among the flower pots. Moving on around, the raised bed planted with salad-makings promises fresh delicacies a few months hence.

"Next, the eyes rest on a comfortable reclining chair accompanied by two small tables invoking meditation. I bask in the sun's warmth, observing the playful flights of hummingbirds, wrens, robins, cardinals, golden finches with their cousins, the house finches and, of course, sparrows. This entire scene plays out under a brilliant blue canopy of sky, bordered by the silhouettes of towering black walnut trees."

Sharing life with Sonja and Ray has been a joy. Yes, we all have had to adjust but, having shared living space with so many people during the course of our marriage, has helped us with this transition. How often I repeat, "I feel like we live in the lap of luxury". It seems that almost all our needs are more than amply met. We have worked out an amicable sharing of chores, with Sonja and I taking turns with cooking meals, for example. Tom and Ray spent many happy hours in Ray's workshop and sharing other tasks together.

Tom and I visited several Presbyterian churches in the area, but didn't find any that even began to measure up to our expectations, set by our challenging and inspiring experiences at Lake View Church in Chicago. Finally, I suggested we look up Linda McCrae, whom I had met in in Guatemala in the early 1990's. I remembered she was from Indianapolis, and I thought she was pastoring a church there. After our first visit to Central Christian Church, the rest is history. Linda recognized me right off, even after so many years since we had shared time together. I had been impressed with her leadership skills and faithfulness, which I had observed in Guatemala, and have become even more inspired by her pastoral leadership here. Before long, both Tom and I formally joined the Central Christian Church (Disciples of Christ) in Indianapolis. We did not have to relinquish our life-long Presbyterian ties! This has become another nurturing fellowship for us. Quickly, we began expanding our friendships at Central, becoming involved, in different programs, seminars and dinner events in people's homes. We found the membership deeply involved in social justice endeavors. Also, it is a community welcoming everyone, including many gays and lesbians. We were surprised to learn of the presence of over forty clergy members in this congregation; some are professors at the local Christian Theological Seminary, others are retired clergy or employed by the denominational regional offices housed in Indianapolis. A wealth of theological expertise is available. The church's mission statement articulates its focus well:

> Celebrating the unconditional welcome we receive from God through Christ, we join together in worship, community and witness to wrestle with deep questions of faith, to grow in love for God and one another, to confront oppression and injustice, and to extend God's boundless hospitality to all.

The Central Christian Church Statement of Welcome states:

> We are Central Christian Church. We differ in race, age, cultural background, ability, sexual orientation,

physical condition, gender identity, family structure, spiritual journey and life circumstances. Aided by this God-given gift of diversity, we strive to reflect God's unconditional love to all Creation. We also know that the church has at times rejected difference and denied God's promises for itself and others. So, we say without reservation: "Welcome, ALL who seek God's life-giving grace. Come as you are, that together we might make a world of difference.'"

We had found our new church home!

The pace of life slowed dramatically with our move to Plainfield. We no longer ran from one engagement with a demanding issue to another, entering into a more reflective, analytical posture as we confronted ongoing conflicts and scenes of injustice around the world. We acquainted ourselves with as broad a source of information as possible. We relied upon primary sources like regular reports from Christian Peacemaker Teams as they regularly report from witnesses on the ground in Palestine/Israel, Iraq and Iran, Colombia, U.S./Mexico border, and First Nations in Canada.

The Middle East Council of Churches also offer credible information about the Christian presence in that area of the world. The magazines, *Christian Century* and *Sojourners*, have been enduring companions for years, and Gloria Kinsler introduced us to the *Yes!* Magazine. This is a secular publication, filled with insightful, positive reporting on different, critical issues confronting our society. Other secular sources include Public Broadcasting System, BBC, and The Day, from Germany. We devoured books on ecology, human rights, and theology which helped ground us in faithful witness in confronting pressing issues of these times. We have intentionally avoided befriending Facebook. We choose to remain in email and phone contact with our family and friends.

During these early years in Plainfield, our grandchildren were maturing, graduating and marrying. We will always remember James's high school graduation, at which his dad was the featured speaker. A tornado warning came through the sound system in the middle of Ray's remarks. Obediently, the gymnasium was evacuated, with us all lining the adjoining hallways, awaiting the all clear. Upon reconvening, Ray picked up his presentation without missing a beat!

Sarah, Tom's eldest, was the first to wed. She and Adam Brokaw were married in Montreat, North Carolina, where Adam had graduated from college. They had asked Tom Sr. to help with the ceremony. Sarah and Adam now have four charming children, Elijah, Isaac, Sam and Grace. Seemingly, in quick succession, Chris and Elizabeth followed suit, with Tom officiating their wedding in Raleigh, North Carolina. Now they are the proud parents of William and Anna.

Between weddings there were high school and college graduations to attend, Paul and Tatiana, Bea and Ken's two children in Alpharetta, Geogia, to four universities across North Carolina. Christopher, Austin, Sarah and Nathan, Tom Jr.'s four. Shortly after graduating from Goshen College in Indiana, Erin married Jordan Smeltzer in Elkhart, Indiana. Subsequently Leah and Lucas joined their family. In May, 2015, Tom married James and Sarah Ritchie, in Brown County State Park, near Nashville, Indiana.

CHAPTER 28

Subversive Seed Saver

The earth and everything on it —
The world and all who live in it —
Belong to our God.

PSALM 24:1

O ur garden in Plainfield, is a microcosm of Mother Earth. Plunging my hands deep into her rich soil elicits the smell of life and well-being. It's easy to affirm love for the garden, and now I know of her love for us. Let me count the ways, quoting from Robin Wall Kemmerer, author of *Braiding Sweetgrass*:

- Nurturing health and well-being
- Desire to be together
- Generous sharing of resources
- Working together for the common good
- Protection from harm
- Celebration of shared values
- Interdependence
- Sacrifice by one for the other
- Creation of beauty.

What better definition of love can we find? I revel in that sense of deep affection while sitting on my garden stool, luxuriating in the beauty of the exciting stages of growth before me.

How appropriate that our new address would be on Garden Place! At last, we lived on a property with space for a large vegetable garden and flowers surrounding the house. As I plant open-pollinated, organic seeds into the fertile composted soil, I leave a small footprint of protest against the mega companies like Monsanto who would nudge the likes of me out of the seed-saving business. My refusal to plant genetically modified seeds in my garden has been my practice for years. Year after year, I carefully select and save vegetable seeds from harvested produce, dry them, then keep them in containers for planting the following year.

January is the garden planning month. Sonja and I discuss what we want to plant this year, then I draw a map, indicating the placement of the plants, carefully rotating their positions each year. We review what seeds we have saved and choose any additional ones we want, ordering them from the *Seed Savers* catalogue, where we are assured of the purity of their products. In late February, my seed starter trays come down from the attic to be filled with special soil. Each seed is lovingly placed in its carefully marked cube; the tray is then placed over a register and germination begins.

Ray built a welcoming structure on which to rest the trays, after each seed has sprouted tender young leaves. As the weather warms, out comes the cold frame, also made by Ray, using old glass shower doors. Here, the fledgling plants rest outside, in the warming sun, until they are ready to be transplanted into their designated spots in the big garden. Sharing with Mother Earth, we give birth to new life.

In the meantime, we have prepared the soil to receive these young plants by spreading the past years' supply of carefully composted kitchen scraps, grass clippings and leaves, over the soil. In the fall, we covered it all with fallen leaves. For the past few years, we have chosen the no-till method of soil care, not to disturb the microbes and worms living beneath. That's what good mothers do, we nurture life and share resources.

Expressing our desire to work and be together, Sonja is at hand to pull weeds and keep these young ones healthy, with room to grow and develop. As a school nurse, her available time to tend the garden is limited during the springtime. Together, we are enriched by the reciprocity of giving and receiving gifts from Mother Earth. She has so much to teach us as well. The stories of our Indigenous forbearers also inform us.

I quote again from author Robin Wall Kimmerer (Potawatomi):

> In the Indigenous view, humans are viewed as somewhat lesser beings in the democracy of species. We are referred to as the younger brothers of Creation, so like younger brothers we must learn from our elders. Plants were here first and have had a long time to figure things out. They live both above and below ground and hold the earth in place. Plants know how to make food from light and water. Not only do they feed themselves, but they make enough to sustain the lives of all the rest of us. Plants are providers for the rest of the community and exemplify the virtue of generosity,

always offering food. What if Western scientists *saw plants as their teachers rather than their subjects? What if they told stories with that lens?*

Among the plethora of species, we humans also have unique gifts to share in reciprocity for what we receive and learn.

Kemmerer goes on to say,

We may not have wings or leaves, but we humans do have words. Language is our gift and our responsibility. I've come to think of writing as an act of reciprocity with the living land. Words to remember old stories, words to tell new ones, stories that bring science and spirit back together to nurture our becoming people made of corn.

Gardening takes on new meaning contemplating this broader picture.

Our labor-intensive efforts are soon rewarded, as we gratefully accept the gifts of our garden. The taste of summer arrives, and we harvest goodies from asparagus to zucchini. Basil, beans, cabbage, chives, cilantro, cucumbers, kale, mint, oregano, , peas, peppers, swiss chard, and finally, delicious tomatoes of various kinds and enough to preserve. See how much Mother Earth loves us?

Summer vacation allows us the joys of preserving this fresh produce from our garden. Frozen jams from raspberries and blueberries and other fruits fill more containers. Our shelves and freezers are soon filled with these gifts, ready to be enjoyed through the lean, winter months.

CHAPTER 29

2015: A Year of Lament

God, find me here
  Where the sun is afraid to shine!
Don't you recognize your faithful one?
Haven't I known you
  Since the days of my youth?
Haven't I sung your song
  In the ears of our enemies?
Why are you silent?
Why have you forsaken me
  And left me to wail in the empty night?
Why do you give me silence
  When I ask for the nightingale's song?
            — FROM PSALMS OF LAMENT, ANN WEEMS

Unmitigated grief and trauma defined 2015. Three important men in the lives of the Gyoris died that year. First was Bill Whitney, Lisa's father, who died in February. Ken Ludema died of a massive stroke in March. Ken was like a brother to my sister Rosaline. Finally, my beloved Tom died on December 23.

Tom's diagnosis of metastasized cancer fell on me like a ton of bricks! Tom's PSA test measured 1600 instead of four, which was devastating news. Further tests showed that cancer had spread from his prostate throughout his entire skeletal system. A prayer by Jan Richardson was calming.

> *That each ill will be released from you*
> *And each sorrow be shed from you*
> *And each pain be made a comfort for you*
> *And each wound be made whole in you.*
>
> *That joy will arise in you*
> *And strength will take hold of you*
> *And hope will take wing for you*
> *And all be made well.*

I shared all of this with our family and close friends. This resulted in an onrush of visitors. Paul and Ken, Rosaline, Annette and Freddy, Pam and Lan Richart, Maribel and Dennis Smith, Erin and Jordan, Gloria, Ross and Beth Kinsler were among the many guests who brought best wishes and comfort in those trying, early days. For my part, I wrote and shared the following poem with many.

> *Where Am I?*
>
> *Between reason and emotion. Everyone dies!*
> *I've lived with the love of my life for fifty-eight years!*
>
> *Between diarrhea and tears,*
> *The former influenced by stress,*
> *The latter still eluding me.*
>
> *Between excitement and insomnia,*
> *The Kinslers have come and gone, with more to come,*
> *With extra work and planning for everyone.*

I'm between uncertainty and hope.
How to anticipate and prepare for the future?
A loving God holds the future.

We all enjoyed Tom's remission from severe cancer manifestations for several months in the middle of 2015. The highlight was the celebration of James and Sarah's wedding in May, in the lovely setting of Brown County State Park, Indiana.

The presence of all four of our children and their spouses allowed us to spend some significant time together. At that time, Tom and I were able to articulate our end-of-life wishes, sharing copies of our wills, and responding to live questions posed to us. It is especially memorable because it was the last time we were all together with Tom.

Tom and I Interrupted a visit with Rosaline in Ann Arbor to spend a day in Detroit with our friend Denise Griebler. We had attended her wedding to Bill Wylie-Kellermann two years prior. He was a renowned pastor and writer in Detroit. Denise took us on a moving tour through the neighborhood in which they live; it is primarily African American. I was appalled by the sight of the remains of a substantial two-story brick house across the street from their home. She told us its history. It had been foreclosed, then torched. A bank reaped the rewards of the insurance on the property. This was merely one example of the corruption rampant in Detroit, which results in poor community services, such as garbage collection, policing, and fire management for the 80% African American citizens there. For me, the most devastating story she shared was about the forced water turn-offs by the city. Under-employed men are hired to report how many homes in which they could turn off their water per day for the slightest infringement by the resident. Too frequently, it was due to an inability to pay a lapsed water bill in order to put food on the table. The church Bill pastored became the center for water distribution for the community. The congregation was receiving donations of water from far and wide. While driving back to Ann Arbor, I exploded with rage at the disparities so obvious between these two cities! This brief introduction to lived poverty in the U.S. moved me almost as deeply as viewing poverty in Central America, I was especially angered by the apparent apathy of most acquaintances in this country. Who is even aware that such conditions prevail in so many areas of the U.S.? Sharing this experience with Tom was important to me, since we had not been together examining the abridgement of human rights in real life before.

Tom and I had become members of the Plainfield Aquatics Center shortly after moving to the city. Water aerobics was my exercise of choice, and lap swimming was Tom's. We tried to go at least three times a week. That exercise proved lifesaving for me, both in heart and muscle strengthening. Starting in February, I began seeing a most empathetic counselor. She also was life-giving to me, helping me manage my mood swings between anger, hope, despair and reality. Tom died in his sleep on Dec. 23, (his mother's birthday), 2015. Sonja and I were both with him, sharing our grief during that dark night.

Remembering Tom

Remembering Tom is pure joy. Two memorial services helped dispel our grief after his death. The first, a few days after his death, was held in Indianapolis. Most of our immediate family attended, as well as many members of Central Christian Church; this was an intimate time of remembering. On March 19, many gathered at Lake View Church, in Chicago, to celebrate Tom's remarkable life. Upon approaching the sanctuary, I was asked, "Look's like a party going on! Where is the memorial service?" Loving words, joy filled music, and a challenge to emulate much of who he was, his faith, and his call by God and all of creation, flowed seamlessly through the service. Reconnecting with people from most stages of his life was part of the joy.

During our 58 years together, I appreciated Tom's commitment to our family, his obedient response to his call to the gospel ministry, and above all, his uncompromising, generous love for me. How I appreciate his wise financial planning, his generous contributions to so many people and causes, beginning with our family.

I will always treasure our shared love of people, food and travel. Our beloved "Dreamcatcher" VW Vanagon crisscrossed this country several times. We rarely stayed in a hotel or motel, because of our many friends and relatives scattered far and wide. Many generously welcomed us into their homes, for which we were always grateful.

Who will forget his love of pinochle? Certainly not his children and grandchildren!

Finally, I am sustained on this new, unchartered journey, by our four offspring. Jim reflects Tom's sensitive, loving, emotional self. Sonja displays his patience, wisdom and understanding. Ken reminds me of Tom's gentle touch and thoughtful expressions of love. Tom Jr. maintains Tom's pastoral heart of compassion and careful planning.

And each of you, dear ones, have expressed such kindness in your compassionate words and presence, for which I continually praise our loving God, always present with each of us.

Thank you for allowing me to share the ups and downs of the past year, and thank you for your loving support which enveloped me with courage and joy. I look forward to sharing new learnings, experiences and joys in the coming months and years.

Tom's remarkable life began on December 5, 1931, when Thomas William Gyori was born to Elizabeth and Julius Gyori, Hungarian immigrants living in Chicago, Illinois.

In celebration of the person Tom became, we highlight his life by listening to what some of his family, his friends and colleagues have said about how he influenced them in remarkable ways.

As his wife for 58 God-blessed years, I feel profoundly honored to have experienced the essence of this genuinely compassionate, generous and loving human being. With Madeleine L'Engle, I say, "And love is nourished through unspoken graces. But O my love, as I need daily bread I need the words of love which must be said."

> "Tom, you have been such an inspiration to my life, which deepened, especially during our shared time in Cuba with the Presbytery of Chicago." — Gary Cozette.

> "Tom was one of the kindest men I have met in my life. His spirit and action live on in us."
> — Mimi, daughter of a missionary colleague.

> "We praise God for your life and how you opened the way for others to follow God's path. The cups of

coffee shared with prolonged conversations in coffee shops in Guatemala will always be remembered. "

— Yolanda Garcia

Missionary colleague, Rachel Lausch wrote: "We think of all those who rejoice with us, but on another shore and in a greater light." (Rachel gifted me with advising friends and colleagues in Guatemala).

"Tom was such a positive part of our lives."

— Chicago clergy friend, Ted Campbell.

Another missionary friend wrote: "Tom used to the full the gift of life that God provided – in humble service, in joyful proclamation, in many an endeavor toward justice and peace,"   — John Will

"Christmas does not seem right without Tom, so wonderfully incarnating Jesus' love, struggles and resurrections."   — Bud Ogle

"I never got tired of being greeted with "Hello, Beautiful!" and I will miss that."

— Dear Chicago friend, Ellen.

John Taylor wrote: "The impact of Tom's time with us is immense. As I continue my journey, I am comforted by having the honor of having shared a small part of his life."

"I will miss Tom and will always remember his smile, puns and pride in his [Hungarian] heritage."

— Dan Swanson.

From farther away, the voice mail of Rev. Victor Hernandez, who lives in Barcelona, and whom we visited several years ago: "We hold fondest memories of our friendship and times together, which have been such rich blessings to us and many others. Receive our love."

Then there is dear Mete in Ankara Turkey, who has called several times, recalling Tom's avid mind for learning new things, even the inner workings of the water purification system he was displaying at a trade show in Chicago last fall. Mete's words, "Consider me your son," moved me profoundly.

Hasta luego, mi amor.

Years of Healing—2016, 2017

Thank you, Adonai, for your goodness!
Your love is everlasting...
  Let those who revere our God say it:
  Your love is everlasting!

                                        PSALM 117:1,4

In April 2016, a flight took me to San Diego for ten days of healing. Lee and Juanita Mangan-Van Ham took me to their lovely home in Spring Valley, near San Diego. Surrounded by their warm embrace, I shared my grief. How pleased I was to introduce them to grandson, Paul and his lovely wife, Lorena. Paul is a naval pilot and they live in San Diego. We enjoyed visiting in their apartment and introducing Lorena to the world-renowned San Diego Zoo. Touring the waterfront, nearby museums and parks was a lot of fun.

In June, Sonja, Ray, Marcia Vierck and I flew to Guatemala City to visit my grandson James and his wife Sara. The ensuing two weeks were filled with renewed memories of our years living in that beautiful country. James was our skilled chauffeur and guide, taking us around the country to favorite places like Quetzaltenango, Panajachel, and Antigua, where his sister Erin and her husband lived and worked. An unforgettable highlight for me, was an afternoon spent with my mentor, Julia Esquivel. She proudly showed us her lovely garden and together we shared memories and current developments in our lives. Sacred moments together. Conversations, shared meals, and renewed friendships marked this timely visit for me.

Tom's Ashes

> *The memory of upright people will be blessed.*
> **PROVERBS 9:7**

After I received Tom's ashes, I decided to sprinkle them in significant places of our life together. As part of the ritual, we videotaped each one. The first place I took them was to sister Rosaline's home. On a lovely sunny afternoon, we celebrated memories of our visits with her in Ann Arbor. Annette, Rosaline's daughter, and her grandson, Freddy, were also present. When I visited the home of one of my children, I carried some ashes with me. In Raleigh, at Tom Jr.'s home, my grandsons Nathan and Chris, who was carrying his son William in his arms, shared prayers of thanks together.

In like manner, we recorded similar events at Jim's and Sonja's homes, each one had its own significance for all present. We had two commemorations with Ken, one in his back yard in Alpharetta, Georgia, and another in Gulf Shores, Alabama, where they have a condo. The latter was especially memorable. Bea, her mother Laura, Ken, Tatiana, Paul, Lorena, and her mother and I, all gathered on the Gulf shore. The setting was spectacular; as the sun was setting in the west, the full moon was rising in the east, as we tossed ashes into the water.

Two churches also received Tom's ashes: Ravenswood Presbyterian, in Chicago, where Tom had pastored before retirement, and Central Christian, in Indianapolis. Perhaps the most extraordinary was in the Danube River, in Budapest, Hungary. There I scattered his ashes in memory of his heritage. His mother was born in Budapest and his father, in a village east of the capital. Tom and I had visited Hungary twice.

The first family wedding without Tom Sr.'s presence, was that of Austin and Ashely, on June 4, 2016. They were married in the lovely Daniel Stowe Botanical Gardens near Charlotte, North Carolina. Another grand celebration of two lives united as one. Fast forward and now they are the proud parents of Micah and Mason. They live in their home in Cary, North Carolina, where Austin is developing his artistic skills with wood-working.

December 23, 2018

"Roses now bloom,
Fertilized by Tom's ashes,
Gracing a patio in Dios Vivo Church
In Guastatoya, Guatemala,

Commemorating three years
Since Tom's death."

When Sonja and Ray suggested I accompany them and Marcia to Guatemala to spend Christmas of 2018, I readily agreed. Not only because of seeing James, Erin and Jordan again, but with the desire to take some of Tom's ashes to leave in Guastatoya, El Progreso. Several months before leaving, I wrote to Gilo Mendez, questioning him about the appropriateness of even thinking of doing this. What did the folks in that church feel about cremation, spreading ashes, etc.? He did not respond until very near our departure date. He finally said he'd consulted the leaders, who discussed it with the session and they'd agreed to invite me to share this experience with them, even agreeing to the date of Dec. 23, the Sunday before Christmas.

We arrived in Guatemala on Saturday evening, Dec. 22. The next morning, James drove us to Guastatoya, arriving before noon, where we were to meet folks at the church. Oh, how that town has changed since last I was there, so many years ago! We couldn't even find the church, nor the house where we used to live (we were a block off!). Sonja and I were excited to be walking around town a bit before meeting up with friends at the church. The session had invited our family to share lunch with them in a lovely restaurant in El Rancho. About 15 of us engaged in lively conversations around the table, becoming re-acquainted and enjoying being with Gilo, Esthela and Ichoqui, their daughter. Before 2 p.m., we returned to Dios Vivo church where between 30 and 50 people had gathered. Chairs had been set up in rows under a tarp on the patio. I asked that the chairs be placed in a circle and that a planter be place in the center to receive the ashes. I was almost overwhelmed by the number of people who came up to me saying, "Do you remember me?" Fifty years had passed since we lived there, only after hearing the name could I remember the person. Such a genuinely warm welcome they gave us! The pastor, whom I didn't know, turned the afternoon over to me. I asked him to open with prayer. After sharing my gratitude for the warm reception, I invited all who wished to, to take some ashes from the bag containing them and sprinkle them in the pot, sharing a memory they had of Tom.

Smiles mixed with tears, as so many told of experiences they remembered of the four years we had lived among them. Some shared of Tom's marrying them, others that Tom had driven them to the capital after their wedding. So few people had cars way back then! Many talked about the impact of Icthus on their lives, and those of their children. Icthus is the youth program Tom and Gilo had developed. Gilo spoke at length of the symbolism of Tom's ashes resting among them. I could not have anticipated a better celebration of the third anniversary of Tom's death.

Having Sonja, Ray, Erin and Jordan, James and Marcia present for this unforgettable afternoon moved me profoundly. Our Guatemalan colleagues, Yoly and Edgardo Garcia had intended to be with us, but Yoly suffered a sciatica attack, leaving her almost unable to walk. Both Yoly and I regretted that she could not be . Jose Luis Saguil, another friend, also was unable to join us because he had an Advent event in a Kekchi church he needed to attend. Other invitees were unable to come for health reasons as well. David and Rosario did drive down, and Rosario later told me, "In Guatemala, we never do anything like this. At a funeral, no one mentions the person who died except whoever is officiating the service." Having people share memories spontaneously, was very moving for her.

Daniel Lopez Solis, the clerk of session, had been my primary contact person with the church. Tom had married several couples, and Daniel and his wife were among them. He sent me a photo of the rose bush, which bloomed after we left. What a confirmation of the beautiful closure to our ministry in Guatemala!

For several weeks upon returning home to Plainfield, I was disturbed by the new feeling of not being interested in returning to Guatemala, a sensation quite foreign to me. One Sunday, after worship, I was explaining to Rev. Angel Rivera how moving I had found the experience of leaving some of Tom's ashes in Guastatoya. He looked at me compassionately, saying in effect, "That experience marked the closure of a significant time of your life and ministry. A very understandable response/reaction on your part." That made all kinds of sense to me and relieved my angst. After all, now journeying in my 85th year, it is permissible to accept those feelings. Another moment of learning.

Aging and Saging

With all my heart I seek you,
 Let me not stray from your commands.
In my heart I treasure your pro
  So that I keep from sinning against you.
                                PSALM 119:10,11

Now at 88, I still don't drive! Phobias and pregnancies aside, I now enjoy my resultant dependency on others for transportation. Both Megabus and Greyhound provide my frequent short distance transportation, each trip having provided many humorous and challenging tales to tell. I depend on airlines to get to destinations farther afield, like Alpharetta, Georgia, and Raleigh, North Carolina. All modes of transport are subject to my ever-evolving understanding of my responsibilities to God, our Creator, and the footprint I leave on the contours of creation.

Back home in Plainfield, on a snowy morn, in a reflective mood, I wrote:

Winter from my Window

Wet, fluffy flakes fall lazily from above
Gently landing on ice-encased branches,
Photogenically enveloping slumbering vegetation.

Open the blinds and see an ice covered deck
Covered with a lethal layer of ice emerging,
Threatening to obliterate today's outdoor ventures.

Irregularly shaped, ordinary stones appear
With snow-covered sea shells mixed in,
Portraying a spectacular transformation.

Metaphors for aging come to mind.

Disquieting dangers obliterated by beauty,
Demanding precautions with
Surprises of grandeur at hand.

Challenges of aging surround me.

Opportunities for new life and learnings,
Physically, spiritually, mentally and socially, undeniable,
All awaiting my creative, willing responses.

Over the years, I have found my understanding of this God has shifted dramatically. In the beginning of my faith experience, beauty was not related to God. Then, HE was unapproachable, inscrutable, omnipotent, omnipresent, omniscient, whatever those lofty words meant! Knowing, at least following God's will, defined my parents' experience and still felt entirely impersonal to me. Jesus trumped God in our theology. I resonate with the words of Episcopalian writer, Debie Thomas when she said, "I inherited a version of Christianity that glorified suffering. It overemphasized surrender, self-sacrifice, and submission to the neglect and even exclusion of fulfillment, pleasure and joy." I rejoice in God, my Savior, who became incarnate in Jesus, who came to show us how to live, love, and learn, as well as how to suffer and die. Again, reading Debie Thomas's words, I believe in God's 'kindom', which "enacts justice, equity, and healing, so that all of creation can revel in abundant life."

My theology expanded when I began university studies. Then I met Tom, whose love opened up the window of God's beauty, love and caring for me. Soon, my understanding of God moved in fits and starts into an ever-expanding sense of God as Creator of beauty. From judge and punisher to all-embracing, compassionate lover and as guide and resource, wise counselor, and divine inspiration. God is my source of wisdom, understanding and compassion. I long for God to fill the core of my being with peace. God became present in the simple, rewarding smiles of our children. Her presence shone through our ever-expanding plethora of friends. God can neither be confined to verbal expressions, nor by human intellect. I make no attempt to articulate who God is, only as I experience God in daily living. God is the pronoun for God.

Tom and I knew God to be our guide into new, previously unknown adventures, as in learning Spanish, both the language and culture. Our faith also matured as we confronted some rather disturbing expressions of the Christian faith in Guatemala. We were also introduced to some courageous, innovative role models of those willing to sacrifice all for their commitment to justice and peace. Julia Esquivel comes to mind. She was a Guatemalan poet, activist, and theologian who blew open my narrow concepts of love and justice. In addition, reading the examples of Oscar Romero, Ernesto Cardenal and Paulo Freire, helped me see how incarnated God can become in humans. Their innovative approaches to learning the Good News of Jesus the Christ from poor, illiterate, campesinos, modeled and deepened the meaning of Jesus' incarnation for me.

Today, God, the creator of the universe, is compelling me to engage more intentionally in learning how to care for this one earth entrusted to us. We treat natural resources as infinite when, in fact, we are reaching the tipping point of their finitude. Our careless and selfish consumption of what the earth offers brings us to the brink of a cataclysmic climate catastrophe. I'm well aware that many disagree with this assessment. However, a sense of this urgency compels me. Hope resides in the fact that there are many, many groups, large and small, actively working on these issues, and my hope and prayer is that the church of Jesus Christ will step up to the plate and provide additional leadership.

CHAPTER 30

Travel as a Tourist

You put joy in my heart—
  A joy greater than being
  Full of bread and new wine.
In peace I'll lie down,
  In peace I will sleep:
For you alone, Adonai, keep me perfectly safe.
                                        PSALM 4:7,8

M y dear friend, Ruth Hazelton, invited me to join her on a Viking river tour across Europe. This is the first time I had travelled for the joy of being a tourist. All of our previous trips had included visits to family and/or friends, or in pursuit of human rights advocacy. On August 16, 2017, we flew to Amsterdam, where our Viking ship awaited us. After a good rest, we spent several hours walking around the city. We saw more bikes on the streets and parking lot than I have seen in my life! Fortunately, Ruth was somewhat familiar with this fascinating city and helped me understand what we were seeing.

As the ship slipped its moorings, we began the most pampered, luxuriously accommodated cruise of my travel experiences! Our small stateroom comfortably housed us, and a good window afforded us expansive views of the rivers we traversed. Before leaving Holland, we enjoyed viewing renowned windmills, a cheese factory and a nearby farm.

Sumptuous meals were enjoyed, reflecting cuisines of the countries we passed through. We met many interesting people among the passengers, and friendships were established. Soon a predictable group of six of us shared the same table for most evening meals. The ship offered many and varied spaces in which to relax, read, and absorb the beautiful scenery as we glided by. Comfortable lounges were gracefully situated inside, and comfortable lounge chairs awaited on decks. Lovely, colorful, villages nestled invitingly along the banks of the rivers. Vineyards, castles, locks, and interesting water traffic intrigued us. Brilliant white swans were silhouetted in the deep blue of the water. Tranquility enveloped us for two weeks!

Embarking in Amsterdam, we stopped daily in different ports along the Rhine, Main, and Danube Rivers. We visited eight German cities and four cities in Austria before finally disembarking in Budapest, Hungary. We were granted several choices in each city, from walking tours to short bus rides to a nearby point of interest. Ruth and I chose the walking tours, with me taking one day of rest in Bamberg, Germany. We learned so much along this leisurely route; it was hard to absorb so much information. A lengthy explanation was given about the significance, cost, and construction of the Main-Danube Canal, linking the Rhine, Main and Danube Rivers into one, uninterrupted waterway from Amsterdam through Budapest to the Black Sea shores of Romania. This canal includes 16 stair-step river locks which change the elevation of 574 feet for vessels to pass through.

Every city had its charm, from Europe's largest cathedral in Cologne to the Marksburg Castle in Koblenz, Germany, the half-timbered houses in enchanting Miltenberg and the ornate palace of the bishop's residence in Wurzburg. A walking tour of the intriguing city of Nuremberg recalled the post war trials which took place there. Vienna was one of my favorite stops. We attended a Mozart & Strauss waltz concert in a lovely concert hall. The next day, Ruth and I enjoyed a lengthy bus tour in almost overwhelming heat, which gave us at least a passing glimpse of this elegant city.

Next we docked in the iconic city of Budapest, Hungary, which held special significance for me. There we sprinkled some of Tom's ashes in the Danube at the break of day. I returned to the Grand Market which Tom and I had visited previously. What a gorgeous place, filled with every conceivable produce, eatery, souvenirs and clothes one could imagine! Aboard ship, all the passengers shared in celebrating the 20th anniversary of Viking cruises, as our captain guided the ship along the Danube where we were enchanted by the brilliant lights along both shores of the river and outlining the various bridges joining Buda and Pest. That evening, some of us also celebrated Ruth's birthday!

On September 1, we boarded a huge 747 in Frankfurt for our return flight to the U.S. We were somberly aware of how young our country is, after having been exposed to the grandeur of some of the ancient cities of Europe. Nevertheless, it was good to return home, safe and sound.

CHAPTER 31

Politics and Pandemic

But you, Adonai, reign forever
  And have established your throne of judgment.
You will judge the world in justice
  And govern the peoples with equity.
For you, Adonai, are a refuge for the oppressed,
  A stronghold in times of trouble.
                                    PSALM 10:7–9

The election of Donald J. Trump as our president was an indictment on our society. Where were the wisdom, integrity, and foresight of our citizens? His manifest misogyny, rapacious racism and bold-faced lies blatantly belied any moral stature. I was profoundly disturbed by the ongoing support he receives from supposedly stalwart, White, Christian conservatives. Fortunately, his tenure lasted no more than one term. Two impeachments and many legal challenges led to his loss to Joseph Biden in 2020. Many tomes have been written, and undoubtedly many more will follow, about the disastrous effects of Trump's presence at the helm of our nation. It seemed that confidence in the United States as the bulwark of democracy had suffered a near mortal blow.

The moral underpinnings of our country were eroding irrevocably under our feet. Then the COVID pandemic struck the globe. Mr. Trump's devastating mishandling of the Corona virus was hardly offset by his enabling the fast development of the life-saving vaccine, which he effectively politicized. This resulted in thousands of avoidable deaths. We grasped desperately to the hope that our God of justice and healing would prevail.

There remained one more item on my 'bucket list' of places I wanted to go, Yosemite National Park. I was excited to learn that Ruth Hazelton had never been there either and was enthusiastic about accompanying me. Lee and Juanita completed the foursome as we drove from San Diego to the Park. Prior to starting that journey, we enjoyed several days visiting some of the spectacular venues of San Diego. Grandson Paul and his wife Lorena were living in San Diego, and we were honored to visit their condo near the center of the city. Lorena, joined us as we toured the waterfront, exploring some lovely, old sailing ships filled with memorabilia of ocean voyages they had experienced many years ago.

Our foursome had reserved rooms in a historic inn on the outskirts of Yosemite. From there, we had easy access to the wonders of the magnificent park. We were literally awestruck by the thundering water falls, the spectacular sequoias, the rushing river and the precipitous rock formations, to say nothing of the quiet, reflective moments beside a still pool of water. How insignificant I felt, walking under the ancient, giant sequoias! Once again, the grandeur of God's creation surpassed all expectations!

After leaving the Park, we spent a couple of nights in Monte Vista Grove, Pasadena. There we visited Gloria and Ross Kinsler and I was saddened to see Ross's continuing descent into dementia. Also, the toll his care was taking on Gloria was concerning. Rachel Lausch and Dave Winters were our gracious hosts for some meals. I so enjoyed sharing these long-held friendships with Ruth. Unfortunately, advancing age began to wield its toll on me.

In March, 2020, I suffered a mild stroke, or brain bleed, and left the hospital days later, just as COVID patients began entering. I was transferred to a rehab hospital for a few days before returning home for a two-week isolating quarantine. Fortunately, I have suffered no lingering effects of this episode.

Convalescence in Quarantine

Below is what I wrote:

*Passing through three hospitals
in the beginning of a pandemic
was a memorable trip.*

*My body was submitted to endless imaging,
scans, and blood tests,
resulting in being hamstrung and immobilized
by a spaghetti bowl of I.V. tubing,
and inhibited by pressure bands and cuffs.*

*The expertise, good humor and efficiency of hospital staff
established confidence.*

*These incredible nine days resulted in my brain
having to reconnect with the peripheral vision of my left eye.*

Enough healing occurred to allow my return home to the loving and expert care of daughter Sonja and her family.

The literal icing on the cake was
a happy birthday celebration
of the birth of my first great granddaughter, Leah.

We celebrated it well-distanced
on my lovely deck.

God is Good!

Sonja's daughter, Erin, accompanied by Jordan and their baby Leah, had caught an emergency embassy flight out of Guatemala, due to COVID. They made a last-minute decision to leave, due to the uncertainty raised by the pandemic. They stayed with us, in Plainfield, until they decided to make a new home in Goshen, Indiana. In short order, they found two teaching positions, a home, a car, and soon settled into a new life back in the States. They had had to leave everything behind in Guatemala but were able to dispose of what they didn't absolutely need. Erin's brother James, who decided to stay in Guatemala, helped them to get necessary items back to Goshen.

Later that summer, I contracted hand, foot, and mouth disease, which left lingering numbness in my fingers. This made it impossible to even type, so resulted in a delay in writing this manuscript. All in all, 2020 became a year to forget, as COVID raged on unabated, leaving no one unaffected.

Our family was embroiled in grief with Sarah and Adam, as she suffered two miscarriages in the year. After burying these two baby boys, Adam had to leave his position as youth pastor in the church and took work as an independent contractor until being called to a new congregation in Dalton,

Georgia. The family made the move during Sarah's next pregnancy and are happily living in their new home in this lovely north Georgian town. Grace Ann Brokaw was born on April 11, 2022, joining her three proud brothers, Elijah, Isaac, Sam and elated parents!

Wars and Weeds

> *God will scatter the nations whose lust creates war.*
> **PSALM 68:30**

The beautiful garden that is the United States has been invaded by the weeds of wars throughout my entire life. World War II very nearly separated me from my parents at its very inception. I dare not claim divine intervention on my behalf when it took the deaths of thousands of Japanese citizens to bring an end to that conflict, by our detonation of two nuclear bombs. My husband Tom participated in the Korean War, which never concluded with a peace agreement. The wars on drugs and poverty ended neither drugs nor poverty in our nation. The Cuban missile crisis very nearly threw us into a nuclear conflagration with Russia. The U.S. wars of intervention into the sovereignty of Central America became the focus of my advocacy work for ten years. From there, it seems we moved irrevocably into the Middle East where we were stranded for decades. Our almost unquestioned military support of Israel in its apartheid overtures against the Palestinians is another "weed" to be extracted. The pernicious, destructive advance of the weeds of war seemed hell-bent on destroying our lush, global garden. The elephant in our room continues to be our on-going war on our planet earth! Praise God for the tireless work of faithful "weeders" who oppose the warmongering and have helped to mitigate permanent damage. What are we learning? What lies ahead? What work are we willing to do and what sacrifices must we contemplate to save Mother Earth?

These questions take on new meaning and urgency as we emerge from the current crises we face. Everyone has been affected in one way or another as a result of the global pandemic, COVID. We've all been "cracked open", as author Stephanie Sellers explains in her excellent book, *The Church Cracked Open*. She quotes Jesuit professor Tomas Halik who wrote, "Maybe this time of empty church buildings symbolically exposes the churches' hidden emptiness and their possible future unless they make a serious attempt to show the world a completely different face of Christianity." Now that those disastrous two and a half years are hopefully behind us, how is the church reevaluating its presence in the world today? The weeds keep spreading.

The ongoing spread of the pernicious weeds planted in Washington, D.C., during the disastrous reign of Donald Trump, continues to this day. The roots continue to entangle themselves divisively among white, evangelical Christians, among too many others. We all know how attractive the foliage and flowers of some weeds can be. The overt lies and disruption promulgated by Mr. Trump were antithetical to the biblical message of love of enemies and compassion for neighbors. What happened to Jesus' admonition of "you shall know the truth and the truth will set you free?"

And then the murder of George Floyd happened. How have we come to terms with the critical role racism continues to play in our society? Challenging questions demand our responses to how ingrained in White supremacy we Christians have become in so many aspects of our lives, including the very structures, observances and governance of our churches. May we not become deluded in how well we are cultivating our universal garden.

The devastation being wrought on Ukraine right now, in 2022, is unconscionable. That Russia, a permanent member of the Security Council of the United Nations, has so brazenly invaded the sovereign nation of Ukraine is beyond the pale of international behavior. My personal challenge has been how to pray for the cessation of war there. Romans 8 calls on us to engage the Spirit to articulate our sighs before God. Many sighs and moans have escaped me during this war. My belief in nonviolence has been challenged. My search for unanswered questions continues unabated. The story of one Ukrainian woman watering the lovely non-native plants in her apartment in eastern Ukraine is heart-warming as she continues to honor life.

A Well-Watered Garden

If you get rid of unfair practices,
  Quit blaming victims,
  Quit gossiping about other people's sins
  If you are generous with the hungry
  And start giving yourselves to the down-and-out,
  Your lives will begin to glow in the darkness,
  Your shadowed lives will be bathed in sunlight.

> *I will always show you where to go.*
> *I'll give you a full life in the emptiest of places—*
>   *Firm muscles, strong bones.*
> *You'll be like a well-watered garden,*
>   *A gurgling spring that never runs dry.*
> *You'll use the old rubble of past lives to build anew,*
>   *Rebuild the foundations from out of your past.*
> *You'll be known as those who can fix anything,*
>   *Restore old ruins, rebuild and renovate*
>   *Make the community livable again.*
>
> ISA. 58:8–12 (FROM THE MESSAGE)

Today, in April 2022, I invite you to join me in our apparently fallow garden. In fact, she is very much alive and pregnant with promise. The surface is a boring brown blanket of last fall's leaves and grass clippings. Beneath the surface, lively fat earth worms are busy burrowing their way through previously compacted clay, but today it has become well aerated by these resourceful friends. In late March, the scene was enlivened by the eruption of lovely yellow daffodils which Sonja had planted, scattered throughout the garden. The confirmation of life and beauty. This barren landscape is crossed by lovely, curving, brick paths installed by Sonja and Ray, dividing the plot into planting sections.

In the meantime, indoors you can see small seedlings that have germinated from the tomato and sweet pepper seeds saved from last summer's seed-saver's harvest. Soon these little fledglings will be transported to the cold frame, awaiting them on my deck. There they will "harden" for a few days before finding their designated growing places in the garden. Miraculously, these three- to four-inch seedlings will grow into flourishing five- to six-foot tall tomato plants sporting lovely, sweet, red tomatoes!

Yes, our garden is our living, breathing model of the fulfilled life God created us to live, so clearly articulated by Isaiah in the passage above. Recently, I have been inspired to pledge gratitude for the gifts that we receive from Mother Nature. In her engrossing book, *Braiding Sweetgrass*, author Robin Wall Kimmerer tells of a primary school of Onondaga Nation children who daily recite the Thanksgiving Address at the beginning of each school day. It is a way of sending greetings and thanks to all members of the natural world. Here I quote the section on giving thanks for vegetable gardens:

> *With one mind, we honor and thank all the Food Plants we harvest from the garden, especially the Three Sisters who feed the people with such abundance. Since the beginning of time, the grains, vegetables, beans, and fruit have helped the people survive. Many other living things draw strength from them as well. We gather in our minds all the plant foods and send them a greeting and thanks. Now our minds are one.*

Kimmerer, in *Braiding Sweetgrass*, reflects on expressing gratitude saying,

> *... contentment is a radical proposition. Recognizing abundance rather than scarcity undermines an economy that thrives by creating unmet desires. Gratitude cultivates an ethic of fullness, but the economy needs emptiness. The Thanksgiving Address reminds you that you already have everything you need. Gratitude doesn't send you out shopping to find satisfaction; it comes as a gift rather than a commodity, subverting the foundation of the whole economy. That's good medicine for land and people alike.*

CHAPTER 32

Rosaline

F our, overgrown kale plants rested forlornly in the kitchen sink. These sturdy plants had survived the rigors of Indiana's winter frozen soil. In spite of the winter chill, these plants survived. Brown, dried seed pods nestled among bright green leaves, harbingers of life. Sonja carefully harvested the kale leaves, bagging them for future salads. These resilient plants served me as a metaphor for sister Rosaline's fruitful life. She died on May 16, 2022. Rosaline planted innumerable seeds of friendship during her 85 years of life. Her daughter Annette wrote:

She loved meeting new people and was known for her empathy. Individuals now living around the world consider her a second Mom or special grandmother. Many people relied on her during some of their most difficult transitions in early adult and parenthood. She hosted many students and other individuals in her home for months or years at a time, creating deep impressions. She was wise.

Catherine shared some of Rosaline's well-known "sayings," as more fruits of her generous life. Some of Cat's favorites are: "People are more important than ideas." "They're good people", "Thank you Jesus!", and finally, "All this and heaven too." Cat brought each of these to life by illustrating how she had been influenced by them.

All in all, saying good bye to my only, and younger sibling, thrusts me again into grieving and mourning, and has become another reminder of my own mortality. The final weeks of her life were fraught with major life-altering changes, including moving out of her beloved condo in which she had lived for more than twenty years. She was more than pleased with the lovely, small apartment which became available to her in Glacier Hills Retirement Facility, where she joined many dear friends from her church. The daily conversations we enjoyed during this transition time brought us closer together as sisters. Her funeral, beautifully planned and executed by her daughters, was a loving celebration of her life, well lived, and commemorated by many of her family and friends in the Christian Reformed Church of Ann Arbor.

With profound gratitude, I am thankful to God, the creator of our Mother the Earth, for gifting me with every one of you who are each being subversive seed-savers in your own creative ways. Thank you for accompanying me on my life's journey of attempting to plant and harvest the beautiful products of peace and justice in this glorious globe we all call home.

Acknowledgments

This writing project would never have come to fruition without the incredible work of many people. The primary editors who meticulously read through the manuscript and made necessary corrections are: Ruth Hazelton, Barbara Frost, Judith Wray, and Lee Mangan Van Ham. Our indefatigable publisher, David Wogahn, carries the weight of getting hard copies into your hands. My soul sister, Juanita Mangan-VanHam designed the beautiful cover. The encouragement of so many family members and friends kept the initiative alive as well. My heartfelt gratitude extends to one and all.

Made in the USA
Middletown, DE
01 November 2022